Finding Inner Security

A WOMAN'S QUEST FOR INTERDEPENDENCE

JANET CONGO

Regal Books

A Division of GL Publications
Ventura, California, U.S.A.

Rights for publishing this book in other languages are contracted by Gospel Literature International (GLINT) foundation. GLINT also provides technical help for the adaptation, translation, and publishing of Bible study resources and books in scores of languages worldwide. For further information, contact GLINT, Post Office Box 6688, Ventura, California 93006, U.S.A., or the publisher.

Published by Regal Books
A Division of GL Publications
Ventura, California 93006
Printed in U.S.A.

Library of Congress Cataloging in Publication Data.

Congo, Janet, 1949-
    Finding inner security.

    Bibliography: p.
    1. Women—Religious life. I. Title.
BV4527.C64   1985   248.8′43   85-14283
ISBN: 0-8307-1045-0

To my husband Dave
with whom
I'm continually discovering and celebrating
the joys of interdependence.

To my son Christopher and daughter Amy
who are choosing their own styles
of relating.

I offer my love,
my thoughts and
my thanks.

Contents

Foreword

There was a time years ago when a young woman with incredibly beautiful big blue eyes pushed her way into my life. Yes, in a soft-voiced, feminine and disarming way she pushed right in and got herself invited to accompany me to a Bible conference where I was speaking. And I fell for her in a hurry! Jan Congo was a darling.

These days she's more darling than ever and we are dear friends . . . and so are our husbands. The four of us have been on trips together and in a small group together. I am now an expert on Jan Congo!

She's a woman who loves God. Therefore you can safely emulate her.

She's a woman who is sensitive and thoughtful. You can safely learn from her.

She's a great wife and mother, a terrific cook (I know from experience—yum, yum!) and a meticulous house-keeper. You can safely respect and admire her.

I commend to you our sister in Christ, Jan Congo. Let's sit at her feet together and read her book.

Anne Ortlund

Newport Beach, California

Preface

Have you ever experienced the shock of seeing all your well-thought-out plans disintegrate before your eyes? Precisely seven years ago this happened to me. Because of this disguised blessing you are now reading my first book.

I had recently left my homeland of Canada, with my family, to pursue a dream of my husband's in Southern California. Dave was beginning his work toward a doctoral degree in clinical psychology at the Rosemead Graduate School of Psychology on the Biola University campus. I had received the welcome news that Biola was interested in having me join their faculty. I was thrilled because I had been a university instructor for the past seven years. After arriving we enthusiastically set out to find a home. We soon settled into a new life-style and culture and a home, confident of God's direction in our future.

Three months after I began teaching, I received word from the United States Immigration Department that I would have to stop. Because I was a Canadian, I was taking a job away from American teachers who needed work. Frantically, we appealed the decision three times, only to receive the same answer.

We found ourselves facing quite a crisis. Dave was deeply involved in his doctoral program, we had two children to support and had purchased a small house with much larger house payments than we had ever assumed while in Canada. Dave possessed a student visa which entitled him to work 20 hours a week on campus, but any of you who have worked on a college campus know that means minimum wage! Because of our Canadian citizenship we could not qualify for American student loans. Neither could we qualify for Canadian loans because we were studying outside the country. What were we to do?

Being pretty normal, I hit the pits. Not only was there phenomenal financial pressure but I was forced to admit that my self-esteem had been tied into that prestigious university job—along with the nice little pay check I received at the end of the month.

From my beautiful office on the college campus I had always said that being a homemaker was the highest of all professions. When I found myself forced to be a full-time homemaker my self-esteem plummeted. Not only did I feel sorry for myself and afraid of what the future would hold, but I felt very insecure about not being able to fit into the mold of the "successful" woman.

I responded by making an intellectual decision to be a superwoman. The Proverbs 31 woman would have nothing on me! She may have acquired her qualities over a lifetime, but I was going to get them overnight. I struggled constantly to prove my value. It got so bad that if I didn't have something concrete to show my husband and children at the end of every day, I felt like a failure.

Externally, everything looked fine. The house was immaculate, the meals were nourishing and often gourmet, the children's needs were met and my husband was happy. But internally I was absolutely miserable. There was no time to cultivate my personal interests. I felt as though I lived constantly for everyone else's approval, under everyone else's control. I shudder even now as I recall this stage. I enjoyed very little. Nothing was ever quite perfect, on my part or anyone else's. And because I was so hard on myself it wasn't long until I was equally hard on others. Why couldn't they live up to my standards?

At this time I was offered the opportunity to lead a Bible study and I accepted the position—not because I wanted to know more of my wondrous Lord or because of any concern for hurting women. I took it because I believed this was the way I could prove I was worthwhile, even if I didn't have a career. I'm so glad I took on this assignment. If I hadn't I probably would never have found the time to be in the Word—there were just too many fires to put out. Very quickly I began to comprehend just how different God's standards are from those promoted in our Western culture.

When I first studied God's Word I really believed that the Christian woman had only two relational options: she could either be a dependent woman or an independent woman. Somehow dependency sounded more Christian and less selfish. Independency sounded a great deal more interesting.

What you are holding in your hands is the result of the journey on which the Lord led me. It is my prayer you will read this book slowly and take the time to work through the personalized exercises in a thoughtful and prayerful manner. Be aware, as you read and question, that the concepts presented and *you* are covered in prayer.

I hope you find the journey towards "interdependency" a challenging and exciting one. We, as Christian women, can offer our hurting word an exciting alternative.

Acknowledgments

It is with deep gratitude and appreciation that I acknowledge the contributions of the following people to this manuscript:

Dave Congo for his extensive theological and psychological counsel;

Joan Bay Klope, a gifted editor at Gospel Light Publications, for her sensitive and professional assistance;

Anne Ortlund for her willingness to review the manuscript and do the foreword;

The numerous women who willingly attended seminars based on this content—I'm grateful for your questions, comments and prayers;

My parents and Dave's parents for their loving support and affirmation;

Jean Coffin for being a thoughtful critic and a cherished friend;

Alberta Smith for her timely help in typing the final manuscript.

If I Love God, Why Don't I Feel Good About Myself?

Identifying Four Faulty Foundations

The young woman walked briskly into the counselor's office. At first glance it was obvious that she cared about her appearance. Her body was trim beneath the attractive outfit she wore. Rays of sunlight from a nearby window danced on her shining, carefully styled hair. Her makeup had been deftly applied. As she lowered herself into the overstuffed chair her body seemed to stiffen and a controlled reserve crept quietly over her face. Slowly she started to share her story.

She was a mother with three children under the age of six and at this point in her life she had chosen to stay at home with them. Her husband believed that family was her first responsibility, but her responsibilities and his seemed worlds apart. He was a pastor, an active man with little time for his family. Everyone else's needs seemed more urgent and important than those of his own family. She felt there was no social status in her job as a stay-at-home wife and mother. There seemed to be plenty of status connected with *his* job. At church she taught a children's Sunday School class and helped out in the nursery when needed. But she could not find joy in service like that performed by her husband because of an overwhelming fear of getting up in front of adults. Academically she had done well in college and had graduated with a degree in a well-respected field. But for years she had been laboring under a burden of inferiority because she felt she wasn't as intelligent as her husband.

What can she do? She is in crisis and needs to make some changes. There is no one to whom she can pour her heart out. After all, to whom does a pastor's wife go when her life is falling to pieces at her feet?

There are many competent, creative, educated, attractive women today who have similar feelings of emptiness, depression and failure. Each one condemns herself for her feelings. And as each one experiences the results of this steady diet of self-condemnation it eats away at her self-esteem until she is left a crumbled mass of humanity, denying her very worth as a person. Is this what the Lord envisioned when He created woman? Definitely not!

What has gone wrong? Have we truly appropriated the life of freedom and fulfillment for which God created us? Is it possible we have let society squeeze us ever so subtly into its mold?

Perhaps you are uncomfortable with the idea that secular society has molded us. Perhaps you don't believe this is the case at all. May I challenge both responses by asking you to pretend for a moment that we have just been introduced to one another. I turn to you and say, "Tell me about yourself." If you are like the majority of women, your description of yourself will probably sound a little bit like this: "I am so and so's wife, so and so's mother and I do such and such a job." If you are a proud grandmother you might let me know that, and if we have a mutual acquaintance you might let me know that you are so and so's friend.

Does this sound remotely familiar? Are you aware that you have used labels to define your identity? You have told me *what you do* rather than *who you are* as a woman. Labels should be used to describe the spheres in which you operate. They cannot describe who we are. Is there security in using a label? I think there is—the security of not really having to answer the question of who we are. I believe secular society, particularly in the West, has influenced us to such an extent that we not only describe ourselves but we give ourselves value based on a summary of what we do. This is a foundation, a faulty and destructive one which undermines what the Lord teaches us in Scripture. Most of us have frequently built our self-esteem on this and three other types of foundations. The disastrous results we'll learn about in chapter two. For now I'd like to tell you about this foundation and unearth three others of which you need to be aware.

Faulty Foundation 1:

The value of a woman's life is based on a summation of the things she does.

Essential to this belief is the unwritten law that says the things you do hold a certain status rating. If, for example, you are active in a career outside the home, your status rating is definitely higher than if you devote yourself to full-time home management. Have your values been affected by this philosophy? Please take the time to ask yourself these questions before you read any further.

How do you feel about yourself at the end of a day when you have scheduled 10 things to accomplish and you haven't completed one?

If, for any number of reasons, you have chosen not to pursue a career outside the home at the present time, how do you feel when someone asks you what you do?

Do you feel more valuable when you are bringing home a paycheck?

In her book *A Woman's Worth,* Eileen Stedman asks the question, "Have you ever given thought to why God rested on the seventh day?" I am fond of her answer: "God rested not because He was tired but rather to show us that in His essence He is apart from, more than His creation—more than His works."[1] As God's children we are much more than what we create, much more than what we do. Our relationship with our Creator God is the basis for our sense of dignity, not what we are able to accomplish. How easy it is to fall into the trap of focusing on what we do rather than on what God did for us on the cross. And when we're out of focus we drive ourselves to do more in order to gain God's approval and the approval of others. Before long we start believing that God's standards are the same as the world's.

The result of our misdirected energies is to create a monster—the superwoman. You've heard of her, haven't you? She can leap over tall buildings, solve any problem, overcome any enemy in her path. And she accomplishes all this within the confines of an immaculately kept house. How foolish she sounds to us, doesn't she? But many of us labor under the burden of being God's superwomen in our homes, our churches, and our communities. We try to be the best possible woman, wife, mother and career person—just to mention a few hats that we choose. We take self-improvement course after self-improvement course. Unfortunately, it ends up being self-enslavement rather than self-improvement. Why do we do this? It is because we have adopted the world's standard that our value comes as a direct result of what we do.

When we find ourselves focused on our accomplishments we slip into the trap of becoming results oriented. Scripturally, results in and of themselves are not necessarily an indicator of God's blessing. In the Old Testament (see Num. 20:2-13) we read about the angry, negative, complaining Israelites. They lashed out with fury at Moses when they accused him of bringing them into the desert to let them die. Moses and Aaron, no doubt totally overcome by the cruelty of the people's accusations, fell prostrate and God showed Himself in His great love to these two hurting leaders. Instructions were given for Moses to take his staff and gather the Israelites together. Then he was to speak to the rock out of which would flow life-giving water, enough for all the people and their livestock. Rising to his feet, an overwhelming flood of emotion must have burst into Moses' consciousness. He had had it with these ungrateful people! How had he gotten himself into this mess in the first place? Instead of talking to the rock as God had commanded, he hit the rock with his rod. The water flowed and the people were ecstatic with joy and relief. Was Moses a success? Well, there was water in the wilderness wasn't there? But only in man's eyes was Moses a success. This great leader had disobeyed God, and even though it brought apparent success it also brought God's punishment. Success is not necessarily a barometer of God's pleasure.

In his book *There's a Lot More to Health Than Not*

Being Sick, Bruce Larson writes:

> Most of us think that it proves that God is with us when we go from success to success. Actually most of us will fail more than we succeed, and the real proof that God is with us is that we no longer have to defend our failures and pretend that we have succeeded. If I'm not defensive about my failures but own them, God can redeem them and make compost out of them to nourish the soul out of which wisdom and compassion and insight can grow. [2]

As a Christian woman my sense of self-worth need not increase if I succeed in my endeavors or decrease if I meet failure head-on. Rather its roots are grounded in my relationship with my heavenly Father. Fundamentally important to me is whose I am, rather than what I do or do not succeed in doing. A high sense of self-worth is available to the Christian woman who grasps the incredible truth that she is created in the image of the Almighty God of the universe.

Faulty Foundation 2:

The value of a woman's life is based on what she possesses.

Do you struggle with a tendency to compare your possessions and finances to those of others? Is your sense of worth found in the type of possessions you have, the clothes you wear or the amount of money you have? Such comparisons always result in envy and discontent and will cause some of us to buy and buy and buy—ever searching but never satisfied.

It is so easy for this comparison game to lead us into bondage to the social status of our friends. Most of us have been there, haven't we! I came face-to-face with this issue in my own life when I stopped teaching college to have our first child. I hadn't realized up to that point how much my self-worth was tied to receiving a paycheck every month. As precious as newborn babies are I discovered that they do not score high in their ability to give mothers needed quantities of affirmation or financial remuneration.

My feelings were a little shaky when a friend would stop by at least three times a week wearing a cute little something she had just picked up at the store. My inability to handle being low woman on the social totem pole drove a wedge into our relationship. I finally began to understand that our society's lie opposes God's affirmation of our value. This knowledge freed me to confess my jealousy and begin to build bridges instead of walls.

As we all know money is both legitimate and necessary. Yet it is too easy for us to feel that unless we have lots of money or possessions, we will be left out or not be recognized as worthwhile by other people. We feel we are not worthwhile individuals in and of ourselves.

As a Christian woman, is it my finances that commend me to God? Matthew 6:19-21 in *The Living Bible* reads:

> Don't store your treasures here on earth where they can erode away or may be stolen. Store them in heaven where they will never lose their value, and are safe from thieves. If your profits are in heaven your heart will be there too.

First John 2:15-17 in *The Living Bible* also warns us against the world:

> Stop loving this evil world and all that it offers you, for when you love these things you show

> that you do not really love God; for all these
> worldly things, these evil desires—the craze
> for sex, the ambition to buy everything that
> appeals to you, and the pride that comes from
> wealth and importance—these are not from
> God. They are from this evil world itself.

Are you tempted to cut this out of your Bible? My feelings of self-worth must not be based on the tottering comparison of my possessions or my finances. If it is I will find myself trapped in the blackness of my own jealousy and in bondage to other people's standards.

Faulty Foundation 3:

The value of a woman's life is based on who she knows.

If we hold to this philosophy we soon find ourselves using people to fulfill our own selfish ends. And it isn't long before we become a name dropper. Sometimes even in our Christian circles the insinuation is made that God is particularly impressed by celebrities or by people who are trying to become celebrities. As a result we walk around either threatened by the status of other people or become a threat to our fellow Christians. This must not be! God is impressed by only one man—Jesus Christ. Only those of us who accept Jesus Christ as our personal Saviour by faith receive God's approval.

The insidious part of this particular comparison is the implication that some people are worth knowing and some are not. Francis Schaeffer wrote a book entitled *No Little People*. I love that title. In God's eyes there are no little people—no one worth more than anyone else. God places such a high value on each of us that He has given us everything He has—His only son, Jesus Christ. Can we then as Christian women adopt the world's philosophy that only some people are worth knowing? Can we use people that way to make ourselves feel good?

It would do us well to remember our Saviour's words, as recorded in Matthew 25:40 *(NKJV)* "Inasmuch as you did it to one of the least of these My brethren, you did it to Me." Any time we base our identity on human relationships we end up using other people. Our relationships will become shallow and the security we seek will transform into insecurity. Scripture is excruciatingly clear; we are to have no part in this particular comparison game:

> My [sisters], as believers in our glorious Lord Jesus Christ, don't show favoritism. Suppose a man [or woman] comes into your meeting wearing a gold ring and fine clothes, and a poor man [or woman] in shabby clothes also comes in. If you show special attention to the man [or woman] wearing fine clothes and say, 'Here's a good seat for you,' but say to the poor man [or woman], 'You stand there' or 'Sit on the floor by my feet,' have you not discriminated among yourselves and become judges with evil thoughts? (Jas. 2:1-4, *NIV*).

Suppose two women fitting the above descriptions came into one of your church groups. Would you welcome the obviously well-to-do woman into your group, would you introduce her to your friends and extend a personal invitation to the next women's luncheon? How about the poorly dressed woman? Would you show as much warmth to her? Or would you only pause long enough to acknowledge her presence and then turn away and ignore her?

> Listen, my dear [sisters]: Has not God chosen those who are poor in the eyes of the world to

be rich in faith and to inherit the kingdom he promised those who loved him? But you have insulted the poor. Is it not the rich who are exploiting you? Are they not the ones who are dragging you into court? Are they not the ones who are slandering the noble name of him to whom you belong?

If you really keep the royal law found in Scripture, 'Love your neighbour as yourself,' you are doing right. But if you show favoritism, you sin and are convicted by the law as lawbreakers. For whoever keeps the whole law and yet stumbles at just one point is guilty of breaking all of it (Jas. 2:5-10, *NIV*).

As committed Christians we must reject the cruel comparison game based on who we know.

An interesting sideline to this pastime has to do with whether or not we are involved in a relationship. In order to be accepted in some circles, we feel the need to be married. In other circles we seem to gain more identity by remaining single.

Imagine a group informing us we are not complete without a man. Some women will begin to believe men are superior and they are only half people. When these women search out relationships they often find half men, for a woman who believes she is only half a person never finds a man capable of completing her. Once this dear woman finds the man of her dreams she lives her life through him and takes on not only his name but also his identity. If this philosophy permeates a church there is an unspoken agenda which says, "You haven't really discovered God's will for your life unless you are married." So the single woman flounders, feeling as if she has no value of her own.

In many secular circles your sanity is questioned if you have chosen to be married to only one man. "How old fashioned! How dull! You certainly aren't ever-changing and ever-growing or you would realize that one person can not possibly meet all your needs!"

Instead of our value being a gift from a loving God, we try to earn the affirmation of our peers by either choosing to be married or single. Comparisons with others is always a dead-end route. Our value has been declared! We should have no part in these degrading games that compare what we do, what we own and who we know. Each of us must follow Jesus individually. The path we choose will be considered successful by some and unsuccessful by others. Regardless, Christ's command to us is always the same: "You follow me" (see John 21:22).

Faulty Foundation 4:

The value of a woman's life is based on how she looks.

The beauty propaganda begins when we are very young. Think about those fabulous fairy tales we all enjoy. They reinforce the concept that says the good girl is beautiful and the wicked girl is ugly. The beautiful one always gets her dream, usually in the form of a man. But the story always ends before we discover whether he turns out to be a dream or a nightmare!

Young mothers are made particularly aware of the beauty cult. That precious baby of yours gets so much attention and so many smiles when he or she is all dressed up. Suddenly the child bangs his head on the corner of your coffee table. Now when that same dear child goes out with you with a bruised forehead or a black eye, he is either ignored or stared at. And you as a parent are viewed as either neglectful or a child beater. No one has to announce to you that approval has been removed. You can feel it.

Have you been influenced by this beauty propaganda?

What would you change about your physical appearance if you could?

How valuable do you feel when your hair needs to be done, when you have acne, when you are 10 pounds overweight?

Why are we so dissatisfied with our physical appearance? Isn't this yet another area where our focus is on what we don't have instead of being thankful for what we do have? What a folly it is to compare ourselves to the flawless beauty on the magazine cover who, by the way, had her hair styled by the same hairdresser who is still hovering in the wings making certain that the natural look is achieved.

Lest you think that I don't believe making the most of your appearance is important—I do. The way we appear is a sign to God, to ourselves and to others about the value we place on God's creation. God, who has given us His son and His Spirit has chosen to reside in our bodies. We are His temple! How important it is for us to be aware of the picture we are presenting to the world. But what Jesus doesn't intend is for us to be caught up in the all-consuming comparison game based on appearance. This sport does nothing but accentuate our insecurities and leave us totally self-centered.

In Psalm 139:13 we discover that our appearance is not a surprise to the creator God. God is responsible for making us. Our responsibility lies in what we do with what God has fashioned. It is terribly important to our spiritual and emotional development that we believe God knew what He was doing when He made us. It is also important that we pause to thank Him for His fabulous creation.

Our Creator's perspective is quite different from ours.

In 1 Samuel 16:7, *NIV* we read, "The Lord does not look at the things man [or woman] looks at. Man looks at the outward appearance, but the Lord looks at the heart." It is important to remember that indeed "man does look at the outward appearance." But it is more important to remember that God focuses on the beauty of our thoughts and motivations.

It's a Fantasy

When we contrast our appearance, our accomplishments, our friends or our possessions to others we are making a comparison based in large part on fantasy. We have never walked in the shoes of those women to whom we compare ourselves so we fantasize what it would be like. When we do this we compare our worst, of which we are most aware, to their best. And we're really comparing ourselves to a fantasy. Perhaps this is one of the reasons why soap operas and romance novels are so popular today. We are basically dissatisfied with our existence so we vicariously live our lives through other people.

When we believe we are only worthwhile if we are beautiful, if we use the right products, if we know the right people, if we are successful or if we are financially comfortable, we are building our self-image on faulty foundations. Subtly we find ourselves looking to other "significant" people to define for us what it means to be beautiful, what are the right products to use, who are the right people to associate with, and what it takes to be financially comfortable. One of the nation's top financiers was once asked how much money he would need to be truly happy. His reply was, "just a little bit more."

When we swallow these faddish opinions, society loves us because we fit its mold. But what happens when the mold changes? Once again we experience rejection based on our performance because it is measured against someone else's standard. What insecurity results! This is a disastrously self-defeating process. We feel great external pressure to achieve and when we don't succeed we are immobilized by a crushing burden of failure and guilt.

One of the most ostentatious builders of faulty foundations is the secular media. Producers bombard women with the belief that their sense of fulfillment can only come outside of the home and that her brain is in neutral while she is at home. How do we respond to that indoctrination? The secular women's magazines tell us how very easy it is to be completely fulfilled. All we need is a little organization and efficiency and a highly competent housekeeper to run our homes while we pursue a career.

Picture this model mother of the media. Her alarm rings at 5:30 A.M. and she leaps out of bed, ready for another meaningful day. She feeds and dresses the baby, puts a load of laundry in the machine and enjoys a leisurely bubble bath while her toddler sleeps a little longer. (The authors of these motivational articles never tell you what the baby is doing while mother is having a leisurely soak!)

While the clothes are in the dryer, the model mother prepares a marvelous new recipe for breakfast which she clipped from a magazine the day before. When the toddler awakens she somehow manages to bathe and dress him, make the beds, read the morning paper, get herself dressed in her classic blue lint-free business suit, and serve a nourishing and appetizing breakfast for her family who has allowed her to work with no interruption.

At precisely 7:45 the housekeeper arrives. Mother has 15 minutes to give her directions for the day, play with the children and kiss them good-bye before leaving the house. She looks well put together and ready to face the business world.

The challenges of the day are faced with enthusiasm

and competence because she knows that things are being handled well at home. Before she leaves the office at night she takes time to redo her makeup and dab on a little fragrance. She's had a busy day but she arrives home peaceful and fulfilled in a relaxed frame of mind, anxious to have quality time with her children and her husband. After a beautiful, candlelit dinner together and story time with the children she puts her contented, happy, sweet-smelling offspring to bed. Then she changes into "a little something" and prepares for an exciting, intimate exchange with her husband. They relax together and then go to bed feeling sexy and oh, so fulfilled.

The articles tell us it is quite possible to juggle motherhood, marriage, a career and your own sense of autonomy. Only after we have been bombarded with this fantasy long enough do we realize the impact it has had on us: we have extreme difficulty hearing what God is really saying. We fail to realize that we have value apart from whether we stay at home or work outside the home, apart from the wardrobe or finances we have, apart from who we know and how we look.

We're Not Alone

Our struggle in this area is not such a unique one. Thousands of years ago, a woman was formed by the hand of God Himself so absolutely perfect that God was satisfied. She was created in the image of her creator, equal to her husband and gifted with the ability to reason. She was placed with the man in a garden paradise. We can only imagine its perfection and beauty. But that was not all. She and her husband could fellowship daily with their Creator and everything was made for their own enjoyment.

There was only one stipulation—the tree that was in the middle of the garden was not to be eaten of. The rest of the story is familiar, isn't it! God's Word was twisted by the serpent. He placed a doubt in Eve's mind about God's love for her. The deceitful words of the serpent were: "You will not surely die. For God knows that in the day you eat of it your eyes will be opened, and you will be like God, knowing good and evil" (Gen. 3:4-5, *NKJV*).

Eve's desire was aroused and she asked herself if God was hiding something from her. Eve didn't have to choose to listen to a lie. She didn't have to choose to doubt God's love for her. She didn't have to believe a lie—but she did. The end results we are all too familiar with—a loss of innocence, a broken relationship with her God, an inhibited marital relationship and God's judgment. Eve left the freedom of truth and experienced the bondage resulting from believing a lie. As a result Eve knew fear for the first time in her life. This didn't have to be the case because in 2 Timothy 1:7, *KJV* we read, "For God has not given us a spirit of fear, but of power and of love and of a sound mind."

Eve experienced the spirit of fear because she questioned God's love, believed a lie and acted on the basis of that deception. Prior to this time Eve had based her life on God's spoken word and freedom had been the result. How different it had been.

When God created us as women, He created us with a need to feel worthwhile. He also lovingly created a way that need could be met. If we choose to listen religiously to the voices we hear in our society, the voices that yell "you're only of value if . . . ," our need to feel worthwhile will never be met.

I really believe that in no other area are we, as Christian women, faced so obviously with an encounter similar to the one faced by Eve. Just like our ancestor we often question God's love: If He really loves me why is my nose crooked? Why am I in this predicament? Why do I have to work? Why am I single? Why am I divorced? Why am I poor? Why am I confined to home? Why don't I know the right people? We don't take fruit off the tree as Eve did but we do act on society's belief system. As a result we are sucked into a vicious cycle just as if we were being sucked into a whirlpool.

Why Do I Feel Like I'm on Quicksand?

The Consequences of Choosing a Faulty Foundation

So you say you're a Christian. You have asked the Lord Jesus Christ to be your personal Saviour. That delights me. But I want you to be aware that just because you are a Christian does not mean you are immune from basing your self-esteem on faulty foundations. It is possible, after inviting Christ into your heart, to build your life not on the new foundation of Jesus Christ and His Word, but instead on the familiar mentality that surrounds you. The familiar, even if counterfeit to Christianity, feels much more secure.

Here in California we often experience torrential rain storms during the winter months. At least 20 coastal homes went crashing into the sea during one particular storm in 1984. What a tragedy! This serves as a vivid illustration of our lives when built on ever-shifting sands.

When storms hit our lives we find ourselves demolished. Perhaps we are even led to reject Christianity because it didn't seem to work for us. Of course it didn't work! Our Christianity must be founded on the solid rock of Christ Jesus, not on anything else.

In the Western culture there is status in certain jobs and not in others. Jesus Christ tells us to do all jobs to the best of our ability as unto Him. Society tells us our worth is tied to our possessions. Our Lord tells us to use our possessions for His honor and glory. Contemporary thinking tells us some people are more valuable to us than others. Jesus Christ tells us we are all in need of the Saviour. We're also told our value is based on how we look. Our Lord puts His Holy Spirit inside us so we can become beautiful loving people. God's foundation is solid rock. Contemporary thought is like ever-shifting sand.

In this chapter I will introduce you to two women who have committed their lives to Christ but who have built their lives on faulty foundations. They are both in bondage even though each woman's bondage is revealed in a very different way. You will meet Gloria, who is in bondage to others and Jasmine, who is in bondage to herself. Do you recognize either of these women?

The Dependent Woman

In an attractive, two-story home in a small Nebraska town lives Gloria, her husband, two children and two dogs. Gloria, who is in her early forties, works as a dental assistant at one of the offices on Main Street. Often, when she is not at work, you will find her serving in some capacity in her church. She has a good marriage, beautiful and healthy children, a career and avenues of ministry. She is also absolutely miserable. Few people know this because Gloria is a master of disguises. Most of the time she is attractively dressed with a smile on her face, moving quickly from one activity to another. People just assume she's fulfilled by these activities. Well, they couldn't be further from the truth.

Gloria's Incomplete Scriptural Understanding

Gloria accepted Christ as her personal Saviour five years ago and thought this would end her feelings of insecurity. But she's been miserable. She accepted Jesus by faith and for a short time grasped the idea that because of Calvary, she had been set free from the necessity of trying to please God. But soon she slipped into a trap. Through the eyes of new-found love Gloria read about Christ's life in Scripture. She decided that if Jesus had lived a life pleasing to God, it was possible for her to imitate His pattern. How quickly she accepted the myth that she could make herself acceptable to God by meeting a perceived standard.

From that premise it took very little effort for Gloria to decide that if she kept to her standard, God would be pleased with her. If God was pleased with her, she reasoned, all would go well for her, for hadn't He said that "all things work together for good to those who love God . . . ?" Likewise, she reasoned that if God was not pleased with her He would strike her with sickness, death and failure. As you can imagine, Gloria developed a real fear of God. She was terrified of Him. She was convinced that He would zap her if she didn't live up to those perfect standards she pulled out of the pages of Scripture.

Let's call Gloria's theology the "worm theology," for she has just enough religion to make her absolutely miserable. As she faces over and over again her inability to live up to her self-imposed standards, she focuses *only* on the sections of Scripture which tell her she is deeply fallen, such as Jeremiah 17:9 *(NIV)*: "The heart is deceitful above all things and beyond cure. Who can understand it?" It *is* necessary for us to confront the truth of those words. The tragedy lies in Gloria's inability to see beyond them.

Gloria has grasped only partial truth. When she looks at Calvary she sees the awfulness of her personal sin that put Christ there. She has no eyes to see that because of Calvary she is greatly loved. She only sees her personal inadequacy and feels worthless, sinful and guilty. Even the church she and her family attend spends most of its energy teaching about sin. Very little is mentioned about the freedom Christ offers.

Due to the Fall, Gloria believes she has no value. She believes the image of God was completely wiped out when Adam and Eve sinned. Today there is nothing of God left in any of us. Jesus is everything and she is nothing. Her total emphasis is found in Galatians 2:20 *(NKJV):* "I have been crucified with Christ." She views herself as worthless and God as one who takes sin very seriously and who constantly reminds us of our failures. Because of this viewpoint it is impossible for Gloria to see or accept God's grace and unconditional love.

Faulty Foundation 1: Identity = Performance

There are several negative results from Gloria's incomplete scriptural understanding. First, Gloria works very hard to earn God's favor—along with everyone else's. To accomplish this goal she demands from herself a perfect performance.

Gloria's sense of value is tied to her performance. She sets tremendously unreasonable goals for herself and exerts all her energy to see those goals become a reality. Prayer, worship, study, church activities and traditions become goals she must reach in order to please God.

When she is successful in reaching her goals she feels good about herself. When Gloria fails she feels she is less than nothing. Her emotional pattern resembles a roller coaster.

But Gloria is not content to impose these standards on just herself. She also puts a lot of pressure on those around her. Since she doesn't see God at work in people and circumstances, she lives with the belief that everything depends on her. Gloria has to have the perfect house, the perfect children, the perfect husband and the perfect friends. Everyone and everything she touches gets caught in her stranglehold of expectation. This stranglehold is most evident in Gloria's emphasis on the "outer wrappings." When you are with Gloria it is difficult not to feel judged as to whether or not you are living up to her version of the scriptural standard. Because Gloria is not aware of how a loving heavenly Father has forgiven her and because she isn't able to release herself from her self-condemnation, she finds it difficult to forgive others. She gets great joy in sharing with you an experience of victory (usually as a result of meeting her own standard) but she will not confess personal needs or defeats. In fact, in times of real personal need she will remain aloof and withdrawn because she doesn't want you to know there is failure in her life. But when she finally crashes into reality, the conflict between what *is* and what she believes *should be* leads her straight to frustration and depression. Recently Gloria spent a week in bed because life got to be too much for her. When her performance doesn't match her expectations it is difficult for Gloria to forgive herself.

Gloria needs to confess her self-defeating pattern to a loving heavenly Father. Instead she spends a great deal of time copying other Christians who appear to be more successful at meeting the standards similar to those she has set for herself. Gloria is viewed as a very pleasing, easy-to-get-along-with person who never rocks the boat. Fellow church members see her as a highly spiritual and submissive Christian woman. Her pastor, the dentist she works for and her husband all think extremely well of her—and their opinion is tremendously important to her.

Faulty Foundation 2: Identity = Possessions

Possessions, whether they be for personal use or for her family members, are tremendously important to Gloria. Her home is a showpiece but she rarely entertains because she worries about spills and messes. The family boat is their latest purchase and they store it on the side of the house with pride, for it is the best on the block. Finances are often a source of irritation between she and her husband but Gloria continues to spend to the limits of their credit out of compulsion. Whenever stress rises at work she finds solace in a shopping trip.

Faulty Foundation 3: Identity = Relationships

Who she knows is equally important to Gloria because other people set her standards for her. Because of her failure to meet self-imposed standards she has lost all sense of personal wholeness and value. It is due to these negative feelings of worthlessness that she latches on to other significant people. Constantly she watches the non-verbal and verbal cues of these people to get clues as to what she must do to be accepted. How she longs for approval and acceptance. These significant other people always determine Gloria's sense of self and she has no idea of who she is apart from them. She has never really gotten in touch with what she thinks. John Powell describes the dependent woman's fear so well: "You ask me who I am and I'm afraid to tell you because if I tell you who I am you may not like who I am and it's all that I've got."[1]

When entering a new situation Gloria will test the waters and then fall in line with the opinions of the significant leaders of the group. Gloria has become a cheap imitator of those who have made it, those who seem to have God's approval more than she.

Gloria is quick to point out that her roles as wife, mother and career woman are comfortable for her. The shallowness and lack of originality with which she plays her roles leads one to wonder if they were chosen for her, however. Let's look at the way she chooses to act as a wife. Gloria and her husband are inseparable. She appears to believe everything he believes, like everything he likes and do everything he wants her to do. Gloria has no sense of who she is apart from him. It is as if Gloria has abdicated all responsibility of thinking to her husband and the significant others in her world.

Faulty Foundation 4: Identity = Appearance

This external motivation carries over into Gloria's appearance. It is terribly important to her that she look as successful as she possibly can. She pours over the latest women's magazines to catch up on the very latest fashions. In her search for perfection she has swallowed the lie that she must have the very latest wardrobe and hairstyle, no matter what the cost. Gloria never feels she measures up to the model on the front of the magazine, however. Most of her conversations consist of a stream of negativity and comdemnation about herself and her appearance. Beautiful Gloria is a constant drag when anyone compliments her—she has no respect for herself. She either looks like a clone or hides behind a smokescreen of inferiority based on her perception that she doesn't meet other people's standards.

Misplaced Sense of Self

Gloria's life is one of external duty rather than internal delight, of external motivation rather than internal motivation, of "other centeredness" rather than "Christ centeredness." She has built her life on the shaky foundation of comparisons and has lost all personal sense of self. She mimics the beliefs, thoughts and standards assumed by those she considers successful. She has become an insecure, frustrated and internally negative Christian woman. The irony is this: it might take you a long time to detect the internal struggle.

One of the positive accomplishments of the Women's Liberation Movement has been to question the wisdom of a woman who builds her life around others. But in their attempts to free us from the expectations of others, the liberationists have moved us into another kind of bondage—the bondage of self-centeredness. Women find no fulfillment there, either.

The Independent Woman

By contrast, the independent woman has more status in our society than does the dependent woman. The woman who "does her own thing" is the prime example of a fulfilled human being—to a great number of people. Listen to any talk show on television, watch any movie or soap opera, read any novel or pick up any newspaper and you'll see her. The independent woman, just like the dependent woman, comes in many shapes and sizes and from many different environments. I want to introduce you to an independent woman I know.

My friend Jasmine is an articulate, attractive, well-educated woman who is a journalist by profession. The day I went to visit her she was working in her oak office, located in a New York high-rise complex.

Jasmine's Incomplete Scriptural Understanding

Jasmine accepted Jesus Christ as her personal Saviour 20 years ago. She still attends church to worship fairly regularly and she still believes in Jesus but she sees Him as not terribly accessible to her. He created her with everything she needs and now it's up to her to develop all she has been given. She knows what she wants out of life and she occasionally looks up, expecting to see God give His nod of approval. In fact, Jasmine's main thrust in life is her own self-actualization. She is going to be all she can possibly be, regardless of what that will take. She is willing to risk everything.

Faulty Foundation 1: Identity = Performance

Jasmine is well versed in the standards society holds up as successful. She has adopted these standards and made them her own. As she talks I am overwhelmed at how she manages to juggle her work schedule with exercise classes, weekend business trips and dinner parties. As long as she is busy she feels worthwhile, so she runs a very tight schedule.

Not only is it important to her identity that she perform well on the job, it is equally important to Jasmine that she perform well sexually. She must keep on her toes because there is always someone younger coming along who might be able to outperform her in either of these areas.

As these thoughts are forming in my mind I am whisked into Jasmine's marvelous library. What an avid reader she is! The written word has always held a fascination for her. On one wall she displays the books and articles she has written and for which she has achieved notoriety. It is an overwhelming sight to see the determination and creativity of a friend displayed so beautifully. She has adopted a basic belief that her fulfillment will happen only as she finds success. And successful she is in several areas. She is a world traveler, an art collector and an accomplished tennis player. Believing as she does that life is to be enjoyed, she tirelessly pursues all life has to offer, grasping all that will bring her happiness.

Faulty Foundation 2: Identity = Possessions

Jasmine's career is flourishing and the financial remuneration it brings to her is evident in her surroundings. One window of her penthouse looks out to the ocean and another window catches the twinkling lights of the city, glistening in the distance. Her penthouse looks as if it has been taken right off the pages of *Architectural Digest*. Gathering possessions has been a method by which Jasmine has found temporary happiness. Once the possession is acquired, she searches for another magnificent plaything which will prove to her how successful she is. It seems to me that she has some of the most beautiful treasures the world has to offer. If ever depression starts to creep darkly into Jasmine's soul, she finds that one of three things will "cure" her blahs—a new male flirtation, a shopping spree or a vacation in some exotic paradise.

Yet even as my eyes take in her treasures I sense a restlessness in my friend. It's as if Jasmine is ever comparing her possessions to others and always coming up wanting. This depression leads her straight to another shopping spree which temporarily stops the pain.

Faulty Foundation 3: Identity = Relationships

Jasmine has been married to the same man for nearly 38 years. Theirs is an open marriage. Believing as they do that one person can't possibly meet all their personal needs, sexually or otherwise, they pursue intimacy in other relationships. But Jasmine doesn't want to get encumbered in relationships, so she leaves at the first sign of a stranglehold. Their marriage has been childless, by choice. Neither was willing to bring children into "such a hate-filled world," nor were they willing to abandon their individual pursuits to raise children. They both felt children were too much of an inconvenience.

Self-gratification is Jasmine's password. She is inclined to change her standard of morality depending on the group with which she finds herself. Meeting all the right people has become a necessary tool as she climbs the ladder of success.

Jasmine worships individuality and delights in uniqueness. Because of this I feel very accepted and free while I am with her. But I am also aware that if I was ever to offend her she would find it very difficult to forgive me.

Once I suggested that we do some volunteer work together but found that she was less than enthusiastic in her response. After all, she couldn't see how she would benefit personally from the activity. I question her very self-centered focus and I wonder if Jasmine will not find herself lonely in the future.

There is no remorse for using others because of her basic philosophy, which she has placed on the wall of her bedroom. It is the "Gestalt Prayer," written by Frederick S. Perls. Framed and attractively displayed, it gives her a boost of energy every time she reads it. To this day she is totally oblivious to its clash with Christianity:

> I do my thing and you do your thing.
> I am not in this world to live up to your expectations
> And you are not in this world to live up to mine.

You are you and I am I;
If by chance we find each other
  it's beautiful
If not, it can't be helped.[2]

As I read this prayer yet another time I can't help wondering about the second line: "I am not in this world to live up to your expectations." The dependent woman exists only as she lives up to someone else's expectations. Is Jasmine, my independent friend, afraid? Is she terrified of becoming a dependent woman or has she once been dependent? Is my friend, who feels she only needs herself and her intellect, tied to the dependent woman in ways she wouldn't care to admit? Is this total pursuit of her own happiness motivated by the fear that if she doesn't use people to fulfill her needs, they will use her to fulfill theirs?

Faulty Foundation 4: Identity = Appearance

Jasmine finds it necessary to have the latest fashions and avidly exercises to keep in top share. But she not only follows the latest fads, she creates them. Jasmine dresses for success and depends on her appearance to speak for her.

In a few moments I leave Jasmine, wondering about my friend who not only succeeds in the competition game, but who comes out a winner in the eyes of our society. Has she *really* found the fulfillment about which she talks so freely?

Only Two Choices?

In today's society we often fall into the trap of believing there are only two roles available to Christian women. It seems we can be dependent women who seek fulfillment through other people or we can be independent women who seek fulfillment only through ourselves. Both are dead-end options to women who seriously search for fulfillment because the foundational basis for each option is similar and faulty.

Our Lord talks much about building on the right foundation in Matthew 7:24-27. We need to stop periodically to reexamine on what foundation we have been building our lives. Have we been swallowing the lie that we are only valuable if we do certain things, if we have adequate financial resources, if we know and have been accepted by the "right" people or if we look a certain way? What happens when the rain comes, if our career crumbles, when our health fails, if significant people in our life walk out on us, when we grow older, when our children rebel or when we make a mistake?

If our identity has been built on foundations of shifting sand, the storms that invariably come will leave us with nothing but collapsed buildings. We will be left muddy, negative, angry, frustrated, depressed, fearful and alone. That's the bad news. But there is good news ahead!

Is There a Better Way to Live?

Defining Interdependence

In the last chapter I introduced you to two women who both base their identity on misinterpreted Scripture and the standards of secular society. Even though the foundations upon which they have built their lives are the same, the results produced in their lives are as different as night and day. Gloria is terribly dependent while Jasmine has chosen extreme independence. Because of the arguments of both Christians and non-Christians who espouse these two alternatives, many Christian women consider these their only options. And more often than not if they do have a choice they choose dependency because somehow it seems more Christian. But they are left depressed and insecure. Choosing independence can be equally disastrous, however. Many of those women end up critical and alone.

Don't give up! There is another tremendously exciting

option available to those who want to base their lives solidly on the Word of God. Your options are not limited to dependence or independence. You can choose to be an "interdependent" woman whose fulfillment comes through loving.

Elizabeth: A Role Model to Remember

In contrast to Gloria and Jasmine, let me introduce you to a woman named Elizabeth. Her hair is turning white. You often see her standing in the doorway of the church talking to a teenager. Elizabeth's laughter and obvious joy from living speaks a message young people seem to be drawn to. It would be just as normal to see that white head bowed in prayer or bent over the bed of a sick friend. There is nothing stale about this woman. She is kept young by the Holy Spirit and by relationships with younger people. In fact, just this past week she entertained our church's newly married couples class in her home.

How they love her as I do. There is a smile on her face and a positivity that exudes from her, in spite of the fact that she is now a widow and living alone.

What we so deeply value about Elizabeth is her ability to allow each one of us to be ourselves. There is a freedom that comes from being with her and an almost unwritten expectation on her part that we will be questioning, changing individuals. If we don't question our beliefs and opinions you can be sure she'll question them for us.

She would be repulsed if she thought we felt any pressure to be a revised standard version of herself. She has seen the Holy Spirit work in her life over the years and feels no compulsion to be your Holy Spirit and run your life. She trusts her Lord to work out His perfect plan in your life. She believes her part is to love you.

All who spend time with Elizabeth come away affirmed

as a person of value—an equal. They come away motivated and uplifted, changed, as it were, by her hopeful attitude and faith.

But this woman is no phoney. She has very real needs and it doesn't threaten her to let you know about them. After all, she had been happily married for 30 years to an active husband when he was suddenly stricken with a fatal heart attack. Their marriage can be characterized by companionship and mutual respect, and their kitchen table was not only the place where many differences were worked out but where people from all walks of life and cultures had been entertained. It was her husband who encouraged her to go back to college after the children were both in school—during a time when it was an unusual choice for a mother. You can understand why Elizabeth didn't recover overnight from the pain felt when death severed the relationship. She told me one time that as precious as her Lord is to her, He doesn't have arms. How she misses being held.

Through the years Elizabeth has come to realize that honestly sharing her needs and beliefs is the only way those around her can know who she is as a person. But she certainly hasn't fallen into the trap of being so focused on her own needs that her hearing is blocked when you share your needs. There is an honesty about Elizabeth and it is appreciated by all who know her intimately. She doesn't waste any time pretending she isn't human. When she makes a mistake or loses her temper she is the first person to tell you so. When you share a temptation you are experiencing you don't come away feeling put down or condemned. She lets you know her frailties and then carries you straight to the arms of her loving, strong Lord.

What a wealth of experiences Elizabeth has had. How fascinating it is to listen to her talk. She has worn many labels—wife, mother, businesswoman, teacher, widow, grandmother—just to mention a few. But through it all she has been deeply aware that she is God's highly valuable and significant child. These labels have never affected her self-esteem. Instead they have been worn like hats that have been put on and taken off to meet needs and add texture to her life. She was telling me the other day that she is enrolled in a course on computers. "The world is changing, you know. We've got to keep learning." How I treasure this precious woman of God and remain ever thankful that she is willing to share her life with me. It is a thrill to have a living, breathing, walking example of an interdependent woman in my life.

In the remainder of this chapter I will highlight dimensions of interdependency which I pray will clarify in your mind how it is played out in a woman's life.

Defining Interdependency

The Interdependent Woman Has a Strong Sense of Personhood

Many women have been affected by the Equal Rights Movement to such a degree that they believe, as do many staunch liberationists, that women have lost their personhood. The interdependent woman is not one of these women. She affirms her personhood.

Jesus Christ, the creator God, left the glory of heaven to willingly live and die on this earth because of His great love for people—male and female, slave and master, Jew and Greek. The culture he entered differentiated between male and female to such an extent that males were really the only sex granted a sense of personhood. Females were less than people—things—to be used by men for their pleasure.

Into that arrogant world came a radically different Man

who treated women as valued persons. He took them seriously. He affirmed their intellectual capabilities by teaching them the Scriptures. He met their social needs by being their friend. He ministered to their emotional needs by meeting them where they were and never demanding that they place themselves in His position. He used everyday examples of women in His teaching, He listened to them, fellowshipped in their company and trusted women to be the first witnesses of the Resurrection. He offered salvation and healing to women as well as men.

Our personhood has been affirmed by our Saviour. We are people who have been freed by Jesus Christ our Lord and we play a vital role in our world. Since our Saviour treats us as people with dignity, can we treat ourselves as anything less?

The Interdependent Woman Views Others As Her Equal

Only in Jesus Christ do we find true equality. Galatians 3:28 *(RSV)* puts it this way: "There is neither Jew nor Greek, there is neither slave nor free, there is neither male nor female; for you are all one in Christ Jesus." There is no need to get an ulcer trying to prove that we are not inferior as women.

In our society we face a standard which says our value can be earned. The consequence of building our self-esteem on this foundation is that some women achieve the standard and feel superior while others fail to make the mark and feel inferior. This superiority/inferiority teeter-totter keeps us slightly off balance at all times.

There are four options available to us as we examine our views of equality. The first might be chosen by someone lacking any self-esteem—possibly a dependent woman.

"I am nothing and you are nothing."

That is true equality but not the type to which Jesus was referring. If we believe that denying ourselves means we are nothing, we are, as it were, worms. As a worm we have nothing to offer God and nothing to offer a relationship. The final result will be a withdrawal from service, relationships and eventually even life. This is the option that leads people to commit suicide.

Another option often chosen by the dependent woman is:

"I am nothing but you are a person of
worth and dignity."

Acting on this belief leads a woman to total dependence on others. She needs them for security, for hope, for identity and for faith and blames others for her lack of growth. She manipulates the situations around her and chooses to be a victim if things don't go her way. This woman has assigned a role to other people that only belongs to the Lord. She is a clinging octopus. In the beginning, perhaps, there are some men or women who find this flattering, but in the end they find it suffocating.

The independent woman's chosen option is:

"I am a person of worth and dignity but you are
expendable."

This is a disastrous option which leads us to use others, almost as one would use a thing or commodity to fulfill our needs. We become exploiters. We are bound by the smallness of ourselves and the end result is a bitter, selfish, critical, unhappy and lonely woman.

If we are sincere about desiring genuine change in our

lives then we will choose the option of the interdependent woman:

> "I am a person of worth and dignity and you are a
> person of worth and dignity."

This woman is free to reinforce and intensify another's sense of personhood. She is also aware that each one of us is in need of a Saviour. "For all have sinned, and come short of the glory of God" (Rom. 3:23, *KJV*). She takes personal responsibility for her growth or lack of it; all of us are "heirs together of the grace of life" (1 Pet. 3:7 *KJV*). Her salvation is not dependent on any other person but on her personal relationship with Jesus Christ. She will reject any suggestion that you must be a carbon copy of her or that she must be a carbon copy of you.

How exciting and life changing to realize, as the interdependent woman has, that Jesus Christ's powerful presence is in each of us in the form of the Holy Spirit. Christ is in you and Christ is in me. Therefore the cookie cutter Christianity is neither Christ's desire nor the interdependent woman's goal. Each of us reflects God's image in the context of our own personality and we each play a vital role in the Body of Christ (see 1 Cor. 12). She believes that she is in this world to become all that God intends her to be and that you are here to become all that God intends you to be. If she can reinforce your growth her own will be renewed. Competition is out, equality is in!

The Interdependent Woman Allows Herself and Others the Freedom to Be in Process

This is the woman who accepts herself as an ever-growing, changing and becoming individual. Because she sees herself in process she also views others through those eyes rather than expecting them to be finished products. Nothing is static or fixed about our lives.

Have your goals, talents or roles changed in the last 10 years? I would wager to say they have. And so have the goals and dreams of those around you. But have you ever met a woman who felt her way of doing things was right and everyone else's way was wrong? The interdependent woman opposes such expectations and uses biblical women to influence her attitudes toward diversity.

There is no rigid picture of a Christian woman presented in the Scriptures; the women who followed Christ were free to be themselves. Mary and Martha had a special friendship with Jesus (see Luke 10:38-42), Dorcas's gift of mercy was well known in her area (see Acts 9:36) as was Mary's hospitality (see Acts 12:12). Lydia was a successful businesswoman (see Acts 16:14-15) and Priscilla felt free to talk with Apollos about his erroneous teaching and correct him.

Not only can we choose various roles (and appreciate the roles chosen by the women in our lives) but we can experience them at various times in our life. When we are in our early twenties, for example, we often feel we must do everything and be excellent in all of it right then. Thank goodness this is not true. We may find ourselves pursuing one career or many all our lives. We may choose to stay at home and raise our children for a certain period of time. Life is composed of stages or seasons, as some have termed it, and today you will no doubt find yourself in a different season than the one you were in 10 years ago.

> The Proverbs 31 woman is an example of a woman using her gifts and abilities wisely and in season. She has been wrongly accused of being a Super Woman, an ideal that none of us can expect to attain, nor would want to. She has

been misunderstood, and we have missed a source of strength if we have tossed out her model. Nowhere are we told that she accomplished all those feats in a day or even a year. She did it in her seasons and according to her needs and her gifts and her energies. She has herself, her family, her roles and her spiritual life in good balance.[1]

What have your seasons looked like? Pause right now and make a line graph illustrating the seasons in your life.

As an example, I will graph my seasons for you. As you can see, my husband has experienced seasons right along with me! I also encourage you to focus on the changes rather than the order in which I have presented them.

My seasons:

single	student	junior college teacher	university instructor	home-maker	author
student	home-maker			mother of 2	director of women's seminars
		home-maker	mother of 1		
	married to a	pastor's wife	home-maker	Bible study teacher	
	graduate student				home-maker
			college dean's wife	graduate student's wife	mother of 2
					psychologist's wife

Now list your seasons:

_____

As you look at your chart, make a separate list of all the abilities and gifts that have been developed in you as a result of the seasons you have experienced.

_____

We are in process and we should be free to prayerfully define our own roles and careers as well as accept the differing decisions made by those around us.

Please don't let the role expectations that others have for you threaten your confidence in the roles you have prayerfully worked out for yourself. Your parents, in-laws, pastors, friends and neighbors all may hold completely different ideas of what is "right" for you. Love those dear, precious ones and listen to their opinions. Then stick to what you believe and are comfortable with unless the Lord shows you differently.

The Interdependent Woman Neither Intimidates Knowingly Nor Is Intimidated

Because the interdependent woman believes she is a person of significance and value and you are also a person of significance and value, regardless of your sex, she does not knowingly intimidate you. She does not try to prove that she is superior or that you are inferior because she believes we are all worth the same sacrifice—the death of God's only begotten Son. She has rejected the lie of our society that it is possible to earn a sense of worth. Her Lord rejected that lie before her.

Jesus was also free from His world's standard. He knew that earning a sense of value was an impossible dream. In the Old Testament God tells us that "all our righteous acts are like filthy rags" (Isa. 64:6, *NIV*). Compared to the holiness of God the Father any action on our part to earn God's favor is insignificant until we have asked Jesus Christ to be our Saviour and Lord.

If identity through success had been important to our Lord, why was He born into a simple carpenter's family in the village of Nazareth of all places? He could have intimidated more effectively had He come from Jerusalem. Why didn't He write books, earn academic degrees or travel the evangelist's circuit rather than pour His life into 12 men, one of whom betrayed Him? How could He let ignorant men crucify Him on a cross, naked, exposed to staring eyes and belligerent taunts? Jesus Christ was not driven by success. Intimidation was not His game.

He also didn't establish relationships with people for the purpose of proving how fine He was. He was friends with a tax collector, an adulteress, a prostitute, ordinary

fishermen, women and those in high places. He shows us
there are no sexual or cultural barriers to God's love. All
people are viewed as living, redeemable human beings.

We don't know much about the Lord's external appearance but we know a great deal about His character, emotions and dreams. Treasures in heaven were the only ones
He was interested in collecting. All the methods secular
society has ever used to measure a person's value are
rejected by Jesus Christ. In the fourth chapter of Matthew
Satan tries to attack Christ's identity, berate His sonship
and cater to His humanity. Christ was offered satisfaction
of all physical needs, prestige and power if He would just
bow down to the evil one. Satan's rewards were not worth
the price of His lordship so Jesus refused. He was free.

We are also free in Jesus Christ. We don't look at other
people as our inferiors and make them our projects. Let's
switch places for a moment. Have you ever had the experience of feeling like you were someone's project? They
seemed to take personal responsibility for your growth
rather than accepting you as you were or resting in the
truth that the Holy Spirit was working inside you. You feel
like running as far away from that person as you can.
When that person is your spouse your situation is compli-
cated, to say the least. Much prayer and communication
(sharing the truth in love about yourself, your feelings and
your needs) must be called upon in this situation.

Because of Jesus Christ we can also refuse to look on
people as our superiors. They have feet of clay just as we
do. Heartache is ours when we make another person our
object of worship. Inevitably people will let us down due to
their humanness and the result can be personal devasta-
tion.

We all have areas where our gifts and talents make it
possible for us to do something someone else cannot do,
but those acts should in no way lay the groundwork for

feelings of superiority. Just as many times we are faced with someone else's ability and our inability in a particular area, but that is no reason to feel inferior. We are each unique and we don't want to be like anyone else, male or female. We want to be like Jesus Christ, and the Holy Spirit will work in us until we "take the shape of Christ" (Gal. 4:19, *NEB*).

Is there someone in your life to whom you feel superior? Write down his/her name on a piece of paper. Confess your feeling to the Lord as sin. Thank Jesus for this person. Seek the wisdom of the Lord concerning how you can serve him/her in a very practical way. Also consider approaching that person with a need of yours.

Is there anyone in your life to whom you feel inferior? Write down that person's name on a piece of paper. Confess your feeling to the Lord as sin. Thank Jesus for this person and for his or her area of strength. Thank Jesus for yourself. Review God's perspective on you. Make a list of your gifts and talents. Thank God for the things He is maturing in you. Seek the Lord's wisdom concerning whether the area that caused your feelings of inferiority is an area where you need to grow. If it is, go for it! Take some classes through your church, the YMCA or community college, read some books, meet some new people, ask some new questions—all the time praising the Lord for leading you into this new adventure of self-discovery.

The Interdependent Woman Is Free to Affirm Herself and Others

Affirmation takes place when I see myself and others as valuable, worthwhile, God-created people and when I communicate this perception by what I do and say. In John 13:34 *(RSV)* we are commanded to "love one another; even as I have loved you, that you also love one another."

How does Jesus love? Jesus values each of us for who we are—human beings, highly significant and of great value apart from whatever we can accomplish. Throughout His ministry Jesus saw each person as a cherished child of God. Because of that perception He focused on their possibilities and potential. He held out hope to them. He affirmed us. Jesus delighted in giving His disciples names they could grow into. Jesus changed Simon's name meaning "reed" to Peter meaning "rock." Instead of focusing on Peter's indecisiveness and impetuousness Jesus focused on what Peter would become.

Have you ever noticed that when you label someone all you can see is the label from that time on? Jane and Sue lose their identity in your mind, becoming lazy and impatient instead of being Jane and Sue, God's cherished children. If you are going to give a new name to anyone please make certain you give them a positive, growth-inducing label, just as Christ did.

Never does Jesus label us as sinners. We are commanded to "go and sin no more" but we are not given a derogatory label. Instead hope is always held up to us with words such as these found in *NIV*:

> "You are the light of the world" (Matt. 5:14).
>
> "You are the salt (seasoning) of the earth" (Matt. 5:13).
>
> "Follow me . . . and I will make you fishers of men" (Mark 1:17).
>
> "Your sins are forgiven" (Matt. 9:2).
>
> "If you have faith as a grain of mustard seed, you can say to your mountain move and nothing will be impossible to you" (see Matt. 17:20).

Jesus affirms us ahead of schedule with positive descriptions of what we are going to become.

Following Christ's example we need, with the eyes of faith, to see the potential for wholeness and transformation in each person, including ourselves. Jesus never waits for someone else to do it; He takes personal responsibility to be the affirmer. The interdependent woman believes that she is in a place that no one else can fill and one of the reasons she is there is to be God's affirmer to those around her. Honest affirmations can soften hearts of stone. An apple a day may keep the doctor away, but a sincere affirmation each day goes a long way toward keeping depression away. We often stand too close to see ourselves accurately. We focus on our failures. How necessary it is to have affirmers in our lives. Affirmations move our eyes away from our mistakes toward our potential.

As a woman, you hold a unique position. You have the unique opportunity to become the cheering section for the people in your life. Reach out and touch the neighbors beside you and across from you. While you are in that office or job remember there are people around you who need to be honestly affirmed. If you are a mother, paint your children a verbal picture of themselves as beautiful, intelligent, courageous and totally dedicated to the Lord Jesus Christ. Paint that picture when they believe it and when they least believe it, when they are 5, 10, 15, 40, 65 years of age—as long as they are alive. Affirm them for what they do, yes, but also for *who* they are—special children of God.

Pause right now and take stock of how you have been doing as an affirmer. How can you sincerely affirm the people in your life today? Before you put your children to bed this evening, will you take the time to hug them and let them know how thrilled you are to be their mother? What about those teens? Do they need you to paint a verbal picture of what beautiful people they are becoming? When

was the last time you affirmed your parents or parents-in-law?

Are you personally feeling a need to be affirmed? Do you take the time to affirm yourself when you're feeling this way? If this is a foreign thought to you perhaps it would help to pretend you are introducing yourself to a friend of yours. Take the time to make a list of the lovely things you would say about yourself.

At the same time you are growing in your ability to affirm yourself, reach out and affirm a friend. In fact, may I suggest that you sit down right now and jot a note of affirmation to someone who is very special to you. Be specific in your affirmation. Describe the characteristic you most appreciate about that person and back it up with a specific example from his or her life.

It is my personal goal to write one of these letters a week. I pray for divine guidance as to who should receive specific affirmation that week. How precious it is to have the Lord's timing confirmed when a friend tells me my note helped her through a specific crisis. Perhaps you would like to make this your goal, too.

After we have practiced on the Lord, ourselves and our friends, then it is time to practice the art of specific affirmations to those we aren't so naturally drawn to.

> But I say to you that hear, Love your enemies, do good to those who hate you, . . . and as you wish that men would do to you, do so to them. If you love those who love you, what credit is that to you? For even sinners love those who love them (Luke 6:27,31-32, *RSV*).

We are able to affirm others and ourselves because we have accepted, by faith, Christ's affirmation of us. We are growing in our ability to see the good in ourselves so we are not threatened when we see the good in others. We affirm others because we know that God has a very special place in His heart for this child of His, just as He has a spot for us.

As the Holy Spirit is transforming us into interdependent women, let's choose to be affirmers by following our Lord's example. We will discover in the process that affirmation of others is one of the most invigorating ways to keep our relationship with the Lord healthy.

The Interdependent Woman Shares Her Vulnerability with Those Around Her

Have you ever felt safe and secure and absolutely miserable at the same time? We all have, haven't we? We search compulsively for safety and security but when we find it we realize we didn't want it after all.

We worship in our cozy, warm little fellowships where we know everyone and their families, totally ignoring the Lord's command to be salt and light in our world. Our conversations consist of being against that which "the world" stands for. We are constantly on the defensive. How much more fulfilling it would be to dare our relationships, our churches and our businesses to be the bearer of Christ's love, those spiritual warriors intent on fleshing out Christ's word to those around us.

Within each of us a battle rages. We desire to risk and yet we fear the unknown. When we are attracted to someone new, do we approach them or do we find ourselves pulling away and waiting for them to make the first move? When we are approached about a new job, a change of location or just a few new responsibilities, what is our response?

How about your mixed emotions when you discovered you were pregnant for the second time? The first time you were swept up in the anticipation of a sweet-smelling Gerber baby coming to live in your home. The second time you knew what to expect: sleepless nights, the change in schedule and all the other realities.

What about the time in your life when your children are ready to leave the nest? Can you send them off with cheer and lots of honest affirmation about the beautiful person they have become? Or do you cower in fear, sure that they won't ever make it in the real world? Do you find yourself strangling them, as it were, with your emotional hold even though you want to let them be free?

Living is risking! My husband Dave and I have a friend who talks about "new normal." He points out that we often sit around waiting for things to return to normal and they never do. Instead we are moved on to yet another "new normal" stage.

Judy Haralson expresses this struggle so well in her poem "Freedom":

Why don't I take it and run:
This freedom to be myself,
The person who God created me to be?

Why don't I take it and run:
This freedom from the bondage
of sin and guilt and shame?

Why don't I take it and run:
This freedom from powers
And principalities, things now and to come?

Why don't I take it and run:
This freedom to soar with the Spirit of God
To the heights of love and life?

Why don't I take it and run:
This freedom . . . ?
Because I've never really been free
And I'm afraid.[2]

But God doesn't give us that spirit of fear (see 2 Tim. 1:7) does He! Nowhere in Scripture do we find Christ promising us security or an absence of suffering. Rather, we are promised His *presence* in the midst of whatever we face. As followers of Christ we are called to leave the comfortable, the familiar and to get to the place in our walk where Jesus is our only security.

Mary was promised by the angel Gabriel that she would be the mother of the Messiah. In our more romantic moments we ponder how wonderful that would be, what an honor, what an affirmation, without pausing to count the cost. Mary, by accepting God's will, had to be willing to be ridiculed. She had to bear the shame of being an unwed mother, to be willing to be misunderstood and to spend her life watching people reject and ultimately crucify her son.

Bruce Larson puts it this way. "To be saved means to be so secure in God's love, present and future, that one has no need to be safe again."[3]

If we have comprehended the security found in God's accepting and forgiving love, if we can truly grasp that God loves us just as much whether we succeed or fail, if we can believe that God's love is a divine gift which we must receive but are incapable of earning, only then are we free to risk. Trust must precede risk. All obedience to God demands risk. Only when we trust God's love can we risk.

When I face something new in my life I can sure relate to these words. "If I am not certain about God's will, I need to fight against my instinctive need for safety and well-being and trust the fact that God wants to give me life . . . ."[4]

Ultimately, we are God's greatest risk because He has chosen to reach out, love and minister to this world through us. God is still risking. We are not robots; we have each been created as unique human beings with the potential to deny or accept God's will for our lives.

I suppose the greatest risk many of us will ever face will be the risk of being who we are. Many dependent women are utterly terrified by this risk because they cannot bear any conflict or rejection. But if we're honest, each of us takes a deep breath when we enthusiastically approach life, as ourselves. After all, we are giving other people the power to hurt us. So why do we do it? Because our Master did it before us.

Jesus was the initiator in being vulnerable. He was open about His hurts, hopes, dreams and despairs. He was the initiator in our love relationship. In 1 John 4:19, *NASB* we discover that "we love because He first loved us."

There is a transparency to Christ's life. The Gospels are rich with examples of Jesus' willingness to let people get to know Him and understand Him. Perhaps one of the ways this is most evident is through Christ's freedom to express His emotions. Because He owned and expressed numerous emotions we are today able to relate to Him and love Him.

Here are a few examples of Christ's vulnerability. He:

> Wept unashamedly at Lazarus's death (see John 11:35-36).
> Showed surprise when met by lack of faith (see Luke 8:25).
> Expressed displeasure to His disciples (see Mark 10:14).
> Rejoiced (see Luke 10:21).

Angered at the Pharisees' hardness of heart (see Mark 3:5).

Grieved deeply in spirit over Jerusalem (see Luke 19:41).

Moved to compassion numerous times (see John 11:33-38).

Experienced feelings of loneliness (see Matt. 26:40).

Jesus was the initiator of vulnerability because He knew we could never love a God we couldn't relate to. Bruce Larson clearly defines how God loved us.

He became totally vulnerable, which culminated in His crucifixion and death. He did not protect Himself from us. He allowed us to laugh at Him, to mock Him, to spit upon Him, to humiliate Him and finally to kill Him. He had the power to prevent it but chose not to. And this is the kind of love that He commands us to have one for another.[5]

If we as Christian women are to follow Christ's example we must willingly drop our masks and games. We must be willing to communicate the truth in love about ourselves. We must be willing to be vulnerable, not to satisfy our own egos or for another's satisfaction but to glorify God.

So often our women's gatherings are filled with people who outwardly look as if they've got everything together yet inwardly are crying out for someone to really love them. Other Christians can look so put together and peaceful that it takes real courage to admit one's own deep need. Yet, if we don't admit our need, then neither God's love nor His love expressed through other human beings can touch us where we so desperately need it.

Never are we called to be anything but real human beings who allow ourselves to be known. Any time you feel as if the cost of vulnerability is just too great, remember that the alternative is even more painful.

But how we argue with ourselves. Our self-talk sounds a little like this: "I'm a Christian now." "I'm not supposed to feel bad." "I'm not supposed to hold a grudge." "I'm not supposed to be having difficulty loving." "I'm not supposed to be feeling depressed." "I'd better not let others know what I'm really like or they won't think I'm much of a Christian." So our guilt grows—as does our pride. We build walls between ourselves and others and are incapable of giving love to our heavenly Father and others as well as receiving love from our heavenly Father and others.

What deception! In Romans 5:6 we read that "Christ died for the ungodly." We can do nothing apart from our Saviour. Pretending we are perfect doesn't change a thing, it only robs God of the glory for any growth that is occurring in our lives. When I am willing to reveal my weaknesses to you, and when growth happens in my life, together we can give God praise. I have become a living demonstration of God's goodness.

We often don't want to be around others because they might find out our deception. But if we will share how God is adequate, even when we are inadequate, people will know we understand them. They will know the experiential reality of the Saviour we are introducing. At that point we will become fellow strugglers.

How honest are you being with yourself? William Kinnaird writes, "Ironically enough, people who have come to grips with their own inadequacies and limitations frequently are more effective in caring for and supporting others."[6] In order to be vulnerable with each other we have to take off our rose-colored glasses and admit our selfishness. We have to stop pretending we are perfect. Only God is perfect. We also need to own up to our mistakes. We must not be afraid to say, "I was wrong," "I hurt" and "I love you."

Yes, vulnerability involves risk but we can risk because we are loved. The interdependent woman is aware that Jesus Christ, who knows her better than anyone else does, also loves her the most. That knowledge frees her to risk.

The Interdependent Woman Is Balanced in Her Relationships

Jesus Christ is the ultimate model of interdependence that we need to keep our eyes on. One aspect of His interdependence was His willingness to be involved in relationships. In fact, He left heaven so that He, the creator God, could meet us where we are and get to know us intimately. He made Himself available to us to such an extent that He identified with our needs and even our temptations (see Heb. 2:17-18).

Just as He enthusiastically entered the lives of the disciples at whatever stage they found themselves, so He enters our lives and encourages us to go for more. His love encourages us and sparks growth in us.

When involved in relationships Jesus was able to receive help from others. In fact He was not afraid to verbalize His needs. As a result the Samaritan woman gave Him water to drink, and in Gethsemane, His disciples gave Him companionship until they fell asleep. He received a donkey on which to ride into Jerusalem and the gift of a meal from a repentant Zacchaeus.

In the midst of His relationships, Christ never lost sight of either His identity or purpose. He did not make Himself responsible for those around Him. Never does He make Himself responsible for our actions, either. He communicates clearly His love through His life and His words. Then He leaves our responses to us. Never are we Jesus' puppets.

Another way that our relationships can be restricting is if we make ourselves responsible for someone else. We are only responsible for ourselves. As mothers and grandmothers we are responsible to teach our children, but we cannot do their learning for them. What children do with our guidance is entirely up to them. And they must bear the responsibility of their choices.

Now we, as Christ's followers, find ourselves growing through healthy relationships. In 1 John 4:12 *(NASB)* it says, "No one has beheld God at any time; if we love one another, God abides in us, and His love is perfected in us." The Christian life was not meant to be lived in a vacuum. We are encouraged to be involved in relationships.

As we rub shoulders with each other we see the need to be committed to one another. Only in commitment to imperfect human beings can we follow in our Master's footsteps.

The very word "commitment" grinds on many eardrums today in this independent, self-centered society of ours. Yet it is only after we have committed ourselves to the God of love that we can commit ourselves to care for others and we can identify with others in their various stages of growth. We refuse to make others either our projects or our heroes. Instead we choose to walk, as much as humanly possible, where they have walked, to laugh and weep with them, to be available to them, to be as gentle with them as Jesus Christ is with us and to be vulnerable to them, demonstrated by our willingness to speak the truth in love about ourselves when we are with them. I choose to back up my words with an authentic lifestyle. In relationships I am willing not only to give but also to express my needs honestly and receive from others.

We are one of the best means of getting God's life and love to others. Jesus is our source of strength so never do we purposely choose to have others become dependent on us. In all of our relating, we must remember that the purpose is for Christ to be formed in you and in me (Gal. 4:19). If we find ourselves imitating anyone but Christ or pressuring someone else to imitate us then we need to confess and readjust. We need to honestly share, with no inhibitions, what we see happening and together we need to get our friendship back to its original purpose—that Christ will be formed in both of us.

Love is the evidence that I am Christ's woman. Only through dependence on Christ alone will I find myself freed to be a most courageous lover who will not lose her identity through loving but will find her God-given purpose in loving.

What Does God Have to Do with My Struggle?

A Solid Foundation for a Healthy Self-Image

Interdependency is unattainable unless you see God, your heavenly Father, as a loving, Holy God. It is terribly difficult to give love unless you have been the recipient of love. During the next few pages let's uncover, together, the truth about how precious we are to God, and how much He loves us.

Who Is God?

My personal standards of comparison only began to change as I attuned myself to the whole of God's Word. And it was during this time that I read a book by Colleen Townsend Evans titled, *Start Loving the Miracle of Forgiving.* In it the author describes God's reason for Jesus:

It has been snowing for 24 hours. Knowing that it had been a hard winter I filled the bird feeder with an extra supply of feed that morning. Since the feeder was sheltered it held the only food not hidden by the snow. A short while later a small bird appeared in the yard obviously weak, hungry and cold. Searching for food he pecked at the snow.

How helpless I felt! I wanted to go out and point to the feeder but if I opened the door to throw out more food he would have flown away. Then I realized that only if I were another bird could I indicate where to find food, could I fly with him, identify myself with his hunger and cold and let him know that I understood and cared.

Our God, looking at man, knew He must become one of us in order that we might know His forgiveness, in order that we might point above our heads to the source of nourishment and eternal life.[1]

Only through Jesus Christ can we as women discover our sole source of freedom. We are free only when bound to this loving God, who cared enough about each one of us to send His only begotten Son so we would have a "fleshed out" picture of what He is truly like. Let's examine the Scriptures together to discover what Christ showed us about God, our heavenly Father.

He is the loving, concerned Father who is interested in the intimate details of our lives (Matt. 6:25-34).

He is the Father who never gives up on us
(Luke 15:3-32).

He is the God who sent His Son to die for us
though we were undeserving (Rom. 5:8).

He stands with us in the good and bad circumstances (Heb. 13:5).

He is the ever-active Creator of our universe.

He died to heal sickness, pain and our grief
(Isa. 53:3-6).

He has broken the power of death
(Luke 24:6-7).

He gives all races and sexes equal status
(Gal. 3:28).

He is available to us through prayer
(John 14:13-14).

He is aware of our needs (Isa. 65:24).

He has created us for an eternal relationship
with him (John 3:16).

He values us (Luke 7:28).

He doesn't condemn us (Rom. 8:1).

God values and causes our growth (1 Cor. 3:7).

He comforts us (2 Cor. 1:3-5).

He strengthens us through His Spirit
(Eph. 3:16).

He cleanses us (Heb. 10:17-22).

He is for us (Rom. 8:31).

He is always available to us (Rom. 8:38-39).

He is a God of hope (Rom. 15:13).

He provides a way to escape temptations
(1 Cor. 10:13).

He is at work in us (Phil. 2:13).

He helps us in temptation (Heb. 2:17-18).

He wants us to be free (Gal. 5:1).

He is the final Lord of history (Rev. 1:8).

As if that isn't wonderful enough, the writer of the first chapter of Hebrews tells us these things about Jesus Christ:

> He is greater than any human prophet (vv. 1-2).
> He is God's Son (v. 2).
> He is heir of all things (v. 2).
> He created the world (v. 2).
> He is Himself God (v. 3).
> He upholds all things (v. 3).
> He cleanses us from sin (v. 3).
> He sits at the right hand of the Father (v. 3).
> He is greater than the angels (v. 4).
> He has the name of Son (v. 5).
> Angels worship Him (v. 6).
> He is the eternal God (vv. 8-9).
> His throne is forever (v. 8).
> He is the ruler of the coming age (vv. 10-12).

The most important thing for a woman is what she believes about God. Do you find the dependent woman's God in the above verses? Where is the condemning judge ready to zap you if you step out of line? He is a figment of an overactive perfectionistic streak and the result of poor teaching. This is not the picture of God presented through and by Jesus Christ.

Our God is *for* us. Praise His Holy name! The God who is beyond us and above us chooses to live with us in Jesus Christ. The wonder of it all! Henrietta Mears, in *431 Quotes* says:

> Jesus is
> God's mouth speaking God's message
> God's eyes seeing our need
> God's ears hearing our cry
> God's mind knowing our troubles

God Himself in human form come to bring us God.[2]

How Does God See Me?

Now that we have wiped away some of our preconceived opinions about what God is like we need to move on to see how God views us. After taking a comprehensive look at Scripture, the interdependent woman believes three things about how her Creator views her: (1) she is highly significant to God; (2) she is deeply fallen; (3) she is greatly loved. Let's look closely at each of her beliefs.

Highly Significant

The interdependent woman truly understands the value God has placed on her personhood. And we all need to see this truth or we will never be transformed into interdependent women. Scripture teaches that we have been created in the image of the creator God (Gen. 1:27). We are divine originals! Even though we do not totally comprehend the wonder of this fact, we are aware of an inborn need and ability to be creative. We also have an awareness of ourselves, a self-consciousness that is non-existent in the animal kingdom. Our ability to moralize and to think rational thoughts all tie into the reality of what it means to be created in the image of our God.

In Psalm 8 we discover that we, as part of the human race, are the highest of God's created beings. With a sense of awe we realize that we have been made a little lower than the angels and crowned with glory and honor. Without God we would be just dust, for God breathed His very breath into humanity to give us life (Gen. 2:7). Then through reading Genesis 1:26, we are overwhelmed by the tremendous trust God committed to each of us when He gave us dominion over the earth. Finally, the great value God ascribed to each of us was declared at Calvary when He sent His only begotten Son to die for our sins. The Almighty God believed we were worth that much! If the value of something depends on the price paid for it, then our own worth is beyond calculation.

In today's world we are confronted daily with people willing to spend phenomenal amounts of money to buy one-of-a-kind-cars, vintage beverages, designer clothes, stamps—you name it. You and I might find it repulsive to spend so much money for those items, yet their value has absolutely nothing to do with our feelings. Their value is found in the hearts of men and women who are willing to pay such fantastic prices for them. In the same way our value lies not in how we view ourselves but in what God was willing to pay to redeem us. He paid dearly by giving of Himself on Calvary (see John 3:16). Scripture also tells us that God loves us so very much that He desires to spend eternity with us (see John 14:2-3).

It should also be pointed out that God not only sees us as highly significant people, He also affirms our sexuality. According to Josephus, the women of Jesus' day faced terrible conditions. The Jewish men prided themselves with the "spiritual truth" (taught in the Talmud) that women were inferior. Yet these same men used women in polygamous relationships and for prostitution, both in and out of the temple.

Into this sinful, arrogant world came Jesus Christ. Here was a radically different Rabbi who affirmed women. To start, God chose to have His Son be dependent on a woman for His birth, His care and nurture. In the fourth chapter of John we find Christ giving the first revelation to a woman that He was the Messiah. He regularly taught women the Scriptures and was not afraid to hold a conversation in public with a woman. In Jewish tradition a woman was not permitted to bear witness, but Jesus' words after the resurrection to a woman were "go and tell my disciples." Many more examples can be pointed out from the pages of Scripture but suffice it to say, Jesus sees women as highly significant people. He also sees us as deeply fallen people in great need of Him.

Deeply Fallen

Jeremiah 17:9 *(TLB)* states that "the heart is the most deceitful thing there is, and desperately wicked. No one can really know how bad it is!" That's not really a lot of fun to read, is it? But your feelings don't make it less true. I believe that Scripture describes our heart as deceitful because we try to convince ourselves that we really are pretty good. When there is something that needs confessing in our lives, do we rush to the Lord with it or do we pull down our masks? *Well you know me Lord, I've got a few faults. But a sinner? Let's not get too extreme now. Remember Lord, I'm busy serving you.*

When I first accepted Christ as my personal Saviour I really didn't think God would have much work to do. After all, I was a pretty acceptable person by my standards. Was I ever surprised when I was confronted with God's standards!

The potential for every imaginable evil lies within each of us. Judgments should not come quickly from our mouths, for given the same circumstances and temptations that others face, we, too, have the possibility of succumbing. "For from within, out of men's (women's) hearts, come evil thoughts of lust, theft, murder, adultery . . . wickedness, deceit, lewdness, envy, slander, pride and all other folly" (Mark 7:21-22, *TLB*).

There is another reason why I believe Scripture points out the deceitfulness of our hearts. This reason is as old as the story of Creation. It is our tendency to believe that the circumstances around us and other people are responsible for our responses to life. This was illustrated graphically to me a few years ago. It was the day before Halloween and our five-year-old son Christopher and his friend Scotty were sitting on the porch swing. Their masks were pulled up on top of their heads and they called to me, asking for some cookies. Since it was only a few minutes before lunch I refused their request. As boys sometimes do, they helped themselves anyway. But in the process the metal lid of the cookie jar banged shut, giving me every indication of what was happening in the kitchen. (Every mother needs a metal lid on her cookie jar!)

When those two precious boys saw me coming toward them, they pulled their masks down over their eyes as if on signal. When they realized they had been trapped in their crime Christopher blamed Scotty and Scotty blamed Christopher. Needless to say, they both had a few moments to sit quietly and think about what they had done. But I was busy thinking, too. How often do I hide from the truth, believing that circumstances and other people are responsible for what I have done? Bruce Larson puts it this way:

> If we really understand the Bible we have to revise our thoughts about heaven and hell. We think hell is for bad people and heaven is for good people. Actually, hell is for people who think they are good and heaven is for those who know how bad they are.[3]

Indeed we are deeply fallen women. 1 John 1:8 *(TLB)* says, "If we say that we have no sin, we are only fooling ourselves, and refusing to accept the truth."

We need to look long and hard at Calvary to see the awfulness of our personal sin that caused Christ's death.

But Calvary also speaks to us of the great value God put on His self-centered creation. Calvary shows us we are greatly loved.

For some reason we as women find it easier to believe in our deeply fallen nature than to believe in the great value God has ascribed to each of us. It is time for us to view the entire picture.

Greatly Loved

As Christian women we sometimes look at ourselves only as forgiven sinners. But in stressing the forgiven part we neglect to stress as strongly God's promise that we are transformed and accepted women. We are no longer just flesh people, we are now brand new spiritual people. Second Corinthians 5:17 *(NASB)* gives us a radical revelation: "If [anyone] is in Christ, he [or she] is a new creature; the old things pass away; behold, new things have come." We are not just forgiven sinners, we are transformed into new creations and are God's very own children. First John 3:1-2 *(NIV)* rings out: "How great is the love the Father has lavished on us, that we should be called children of God! And that is what we are! . . . Dear friends, now we are children of God."

There is a radical difference between human birth and spiritual birth. When a precious new child enters the world, the life-giving cord joining the mother and child is cut. Never again will the child depend on his mother in the same way. When Christ gives us the umbilical cord of spiritual birth (see 1 John 3:9), that cord is never severed. Not only is God always around us, Christ is *in* us.

Abundant life and freedom comes only as we are dependent on God for everything. So not only are we forgiven sinners we are also "new creatures" with God in us. At the same time we are in God (see John 14:20 and Gal.

2:20). Can we grasp the wonder of God's truth?

A woman who only believes she is forgiven focuses heavily on her performance rather than on her Lord. If we only believe we are forgiven, then we can be easily discouraged after confessing the same area over and over again. What one of us hasn't experienced that? We begin to wonder if God has lost patience with us. And it isn't very long until we question whether He'll accept us any longer.

Security is not discovered in forgiveness alone. Security is only found when we accept what Jesus Christ has done. When you have really understood this truth you will no longer sit in a communion service, focusing on the awfulness of your personal sin. You will focus on God's fantastic grace and love.

There are no risks involved in God's love—none whatsoever. God accepts us in Jesus Christ, not because of our performance, but because of Christ's shed blood. The pressure is off, dear women. If we understand the meaning of grace, our defeats and failures should not cause us to turn away from God. They should cause us to turn towards Him in confession, praise and thanksgiving.

Ephesians 1:6, *KJV* points out that "we are accepted in the beloved." Because God is holy He can only accept perfection. Other than Jesus Christ, none of us is perfect, regardless of how much effort we put into trying to become perfect. Christ alone is acceptable to God. Because we have been covered by Jesus' shed blood (see Gal. 3:27) and He indwells us, we are completely accepted by the Almighty God. We are not *just* forgiven sinners! We are not *merely* forgiven sinners. In God's eyes we are received and treated—accepted—as if we are Jesus, because of Christ's shed blood.

There is a fantastic word picture of this truth found in Exodus 11:4-6. The death angel is going to pass over all the homes in Egypt, killing the firstborn in each home unless blood has been sprinkled over the doorpost of that home. What if some well-meaning, perfectionist woman had posted a list describing what a beautiful person she was, the activities all members of the home were involved in and the kindnesses they had done? The death angel would have struck that home bringing death and terror with him. It was the blood that made them acceptable and so it is today. We gain acceptance in God's eyes only because of Christ's shed blood.

That is why I can confidently write this message: Regardless of your past mistakes or failures, if Jesus Christ is your personal Saviour, God looks at each one of you and says, "You are my beloved daughter and I am pleased with you." It is time to take off the backpack of confessed guilt so many of us allow to weigh us down. We are indeed forgiven, accepted and loved women.

One day I saw a two-sided poster and the potency of its message stopped me in my tracks. One side of the poster said: "World's view: I love you, I love you not." As you can guess there was a picture of a beautiful child picking the petals off a daisy. On the other side of the poster it said: "God's view: I love you, I love you, I love you . . . "

So it is. In God's eyes we are beautiful because of Jesus Christ's shed blood. The interdependent woman realizes it is impossible to love and enjoy herself until she has really learned to know and love her creator. When she loves God she learns to love herself, from His perspective.

She believes three truths about herself—she is highly significant, deeply fallen and greatly loved. Her true sense of worth comes in her awareness that she is loved and accepted unconditionally. This realization changes her focus from her mistakes and performance to the beauty of God's love and grace. She is freed from trying to please God and living her life through others, like the dependent woman does. She is also free to take off her masks and to stop pretending she can make it totally on her own like the independent woman does. The interdependent woman is the only person free to be herself because she is aware of who her wonderful God is.

It's a Process

Let me hasten to tell you that becoming an interdependent woman is a process. One does not go to bed one evening and wake up the next morning a new person. How nice that would be! There is no growth without risk and struggle. So it is in our search for interdependency.

This book hasn't been written by someone who has supposedly made it. I am not a signed, sealed and delivered interdependent woman. Rather, I am in the process of being transformed by the Holy Spirit. I have had to face and experience both the counterfeit options of dependency and independency before I could realize what shams they both are.

I see freedom at the end of my process. Before, all I faced was bondage, either to myself or to someone else. Even though I slip back periodically into both roles it happens less and less as I truly become a new creation. I'm thankful the process has started because I don't want to settle for bondage again. Won't you join me as I pray the Holy Spirit will create us both into interdependent women?

> Yes, it is true that when you stand before the
>   Lord to ask His forgiveness,
> Your dress is ragged and tattered because of
>   ugly sins,
> Your hair is thickly tangled with the web of
>   rebellion,

Your shoes are torn and muddy by your past
    failures.
But God never sees any of that!
He sees you Holy,
He sees you perfect
Because you are dressed in His righteousness
And He has covered you with the full length
    cape of His love.
He sees nothing else!
Even when you explain how you really look
    underneath,
He hears but He forgets forever.
The dimension of His forgetfulness is as far as
    the East is from the West,
And it endures past all eternity. [4]

How Can I Love Myself?

Beginning the Process

As we express our willingness to become interdependent, the Holy Spirit will take each of us on a personal journey. With His direction let us begin the process of loving ourselves.

Step 1:
Start a Relationship with the God of Love

Many of us have difficulty understanding or even desiring a relationship with God, the Father, because of a painful relationship we have experienced with our earthly fathers. God is not like our earthly fathers! Who of us has a perfect parent or is a perfect parent? Not one of us!

It is essential to our belief in a loving God that we differentiate between our earthly father and our heavenly Father. It is also necessary to forgive our father of any pain he may have caused us. If we refuse, then any time we hear God referred to as Father, we will be overwhelmed by feelings of bitterness, repulsion, anger and perhaps even hate. When our pain is too intense it is impossible to turn towards our loving, heavenly Father with adoration, worship, obedience and praise. We will have great difficulty believing that God views us as highly significant or greatly loved women. Like the dependent person, we will see our deeply fallen nature.

It is almost impossible to love and enjoy ourselves until we have really learned to love and enjoy our Creator. We can't be a better Christian woman than our perspective of God will allow. When we love God we learn to love ourselves from His perspective. Is it possible we have thoughts, ideas and concepts of God that are unworthy of Him because of our painful associations with the word "father"?

There is a person in my life who was severely beaten as a child and who faced more anger than affection from her father. Rarely, if ever, were words of love or affirmation expressed. It was incomprehensible to my friend that God, who was her heavenly Father, could be anything but an angry and vengeful figure.

My friend's eyes were blinded to God's love, grace and forgiveness until she asked the Holy Spirit to walk back through her past with her. Likewise, it wasn't until she was willing to forgive her father (even though this parent still justifies his behavior) and search the Scriptures for clues as to what God's character is really like, that her life began to change. Over a period of time she was finally able to replace her personal experience with the word "father" with Scripture's definition of God as Father. During this time she found Dick Dickinson's paraphrase of 1 Corinthians 13:4-7 extremely helpful in redefining what God the Father is like:

> Because God loves me, He is slow to lose patience with me.
>
> Because God loves me, He takes the circumstances of my life and uses them in a constructive way for my growth.
>
> Because God loves me, He does not treat me as an object to be possessed and manipulated.
>
> Because God loves me, He has no need to impress me with how great and powerful He is because *He is God.* Nor does He belittle me as His child in order to show me how important He is.
>
> Because God loves me, He is for me. He wants to see me mature and develop in His love.
>
> Because God loves me, He does not send down His wrath on every little mistake I make of which there are many.
>
> Because God loves me, He does not keep score of all my sins and then beat me over the head with them whenever He gets the chance.
>
> Because God loves me, He is deeply grieved when I do not walk in the ways that please Him because He sees this as evidence that I don't trust Him and love Him as I should.
>
> Because God loves me, He rejoices when I experience His power and strength and stand

up under the pressures of life for His name's sake.

Because God loves me, He keeps on working patiently with me even when I feel like giving up and can't see why He doesn't give up with me, too.

Because God loves me, He keeps on trusting me when at times I don't even trust myself.

Because God loves me, He never says there is no hope for me, rather, He patiently works with me, loves me and disciplines me in such a way that it is hard for me to understand the depth of His concern for me.

Because God loves me, He never forsakes me even though many of my friends might.[1]

It is this same heavenly Father who invites us to come to Him by faith, believing that He will accept us, as we are, into His family. We don't have to earn His acceptance on the basis of our performance, our acquaintances, our possessions, our beauty or our marital status. In John 3:17 we learn that God didn't come into this world to condemn the world but to save and free the world.

It is this same God who sees us as highly significant and greatly loved even though He knows we are deeply fallen women. If you had been the only person on the face of this earth, God would still have sent His Son to die for you. You are that valuable to Him.

Have you asked this Jesus, the risen Christ, to be your personal Saviour? Have you exchanged your concept of an earthly, imperfect father, for the scriptural description of God as a loving, perfect Father? If you choose to begin with a God of love, God will give you the right to become a child of God (read John 1:12-13). Because of what Jesus did on Calvary, you are loved, accepted and viewed as perfect by the very God of the universe. You are, from this moment on, dressed in Jesus' righteousness. You come from greatness!

Step 2:
Acknowledge that Knowing Jesus Christ Is Foundational to Your Search for Wholeness and Esteem

Maurice Wagner has written a thought-provoking book called *The Sensation of Being Someone.* In it he points out that we all need to feel we belong, we are of value, and that we can achieve, if we are to experience a healthy self-esteem. It was thrilling for me to realize that my relationship with Jesus Christ meets my needs in all three of these areas.

Because of what God the Father did by giving us His only begotten and unique Son, I know the security that is a result of belonging. Based on the Word of God I know I am a child of God (see 1 John 3:1 and John 1:12); I have been accepted in the beloved (see Eph. 1:6) and I am a new creature (see 2 Cor. 5:17). I have become part of a wonderful support group, the Body of Christ (see 1 Cor. 12:27). When anyone in my group is suffering I feel pain and when they rejoice, I rejoice. The people in this Body of Christ are the ones with whom I will spend eternity. I can be confident of this truth because in John 14:2-3, Jesus promises to prepare a place for me. When this life is over I can spend eternity with Him and with the other precious Christians I have learned to love here on earth.

Not only do I experience love, support and acceptance

from God and from the Body, as a result of making Jesus Christ my Saviour, I also have a sense of being a person of value who is cherished and respected. Romans 5:8 *(NASB)* shows me that God's love for me is not based on my performance: "But God demonstrates His own love toward us, in that while we were yet sinners, Christ died for us." I have absolutely no possibility of earning God's favor and yet He sent His only begotten Son to earth to die for me. I know I am valued apart from what I can do! I am now at peace with my God, who views me as His beloved daughter.

As if that isn't wonderful enough, God's love also fulfills my need for achievement. When Jesus was here on earth, willingly imprisoned in our humanity, He acknowledged the impossibility of human beings living the Christian life apart from supernatural intervention. He knew He had dreams to give us that would be absolutely impossible without Him. So the Holy Spirit was sent to do the Father's work in each one of us. We have a confidence, based on Philippians 1:6, that as long as we're willing, the Holy Spirit is going to keep us growing.

Why? In Ephesians 2:10 we discover that God wants us to accomplish good works—that is why He is at work in each one of us. The perfect plan involves women who are full of God Himself and who have the arms to hug the people in their world, the ears to listen to the joys and sorrows of their world, the hands to help those around them, the mind through which Christ thinks and the mouth to speak words of comfort, wisdom and hope.

Accepting Jesus Christ as my personal Saviour means I experience the security that results from knowing I belong and am a valuable and competent human being. Now I achieve, not to get a sense of adequacy, but out of an awareness of adequacy. "I can do all things through Him who strengthens me" (Phil. 4:13, *NASB*).

Step 3:
Affirm that You Are First Class Quality

There are stores in Southern California which make a successful business out of marketing seconds and last year's merchandise. You are not a second, however. You are first quality!

> Let us make man in our image, according to our likeness . . . . And God created man in His own image, in the image of God He created him; male and female He created them (Gen. 1:26-27, *NASB*).

You were created in God's image as a woman. It is true that sin has entered the picture but sin only distorts God's image, it does not wipe it out. In 1 Corinthians 11:7 we read that the Christians at Corinth were referred to as the image and glory of God. Given their quarrelsome, boastful, immoral and immature attitudes and actions, that is an amazing statement!

Have you ever taken a trip on a train, boat or plane? Were you rejected—not allowed on board—because you were feeling depressed, unworthy or unattractive? Of course not. There is only one thing that is essential for your journey and that is the ticket. If you have a ticket you can feel angry, happy, excited or frustrated and you will not be denied admittance aboard. Think of the implications. If God, whose standards are perfect, has accepted us, why do we refuse to accept ourselves?

God accepts us not because of our performance or feelings but because of Christ's shed blood. If you have confessed your inability to run your own life plus your need of a Saviour and Lord, you are accepted in God the Father's eyes. He sees you as holy and perfect and dressed in His righteousness. You don't have to prove that you are valuable anymore. You *are* valuable!

Step 4:
Accept Your Humanity

Are you often aware of your humanity, your frailties? Great! You are earthen and that's the way God meant it when He created you. Second Corinthians 4:7 *(NASB)* explains why: "But we have this treasure in earthen vessels, that the surpassing greatness of the power may be of God and not from ourselves." The beauty of Jesus becomes evident to those around us through our humanity. Is it really okay to be human? Yes! Because Jesus the Creator God of the universe chose to be fully human.

Being human means we have mental and physical weaknesses; it means we experience energy limitations; it means we have needs and it means we have a mixture of emotions. Being human also means we have a need to love and be loved and to feel we are significant persons. We will not be able to do everything we want to do or everything everyone else wants us to do. The great news is that God indwells our humanity so His beauty will show forth in us.

What happens when we forget or deny that we are human? We play God and our perfectionistic and super-woman complex glares us straight in the eye. Like Avis, we try harder. But the reality is this: trying harder can never change us from earthen vessels into deity.

Pause in your reading for a moment and make a list of all the shoulds you put on yourself every day. Perhaps your list starts with "I should lose weight," "I should always be engaged in constructive activity," "I should always be happy," or "I should be a good housekeeper."

After you have made your list, reread it and see if you can remember where each particular "should" originated. Did it come from your family, society, your church, your work, Scripture or your own high expectations for yourself? Now go back over the list and decide which "shoulds" you choose to keep and those that need to be dropped. Work hard in the next few weeks at dropping all the shoulds in your vocabulary, for they push personal guilt buttons when we can't consistently live up to them.

The word "should" causes us to feel as if someone outside is controlling you. Replace the word "should" with the word "choose" and you will assume personal responsibility for your own actions. Your choices will be your own rather than someone else's.

A hypocrite is someone who passes herself off as being perfect. It is not someone who doesn't live up to her own standards or we'd all be either hypocrites or women with extremely low standards. *God* is perfect! *We* are human! Affirm your humanity.

I am loved and accepted by God therefore I don't have to reject my own humanity in order to prove my value. I am human and my greatest desire is that the beauty of Jesus will be seen in me.

Step 5:
Celebrate Your Uniqueness and Stop Asking "What if . . . ?"

Each of us is a divine original! We are the creative expression of a loving God. Think what it would cost to buy an original by a famous dress designer. We often fail to focus on the beauty of our design because we are too busy focusing on why our design isn't like someone else's!

What do you feel when you stand on the beach, watching the beauty, power and immensity of the sea? Do you take the time to meditate on the vastness of our universe? When was the last time you focused on the beauty of a flower? How can we feel awestruck by all the rest of God's creation and still have the nerve to downgrade ourselves?

You and I have unique talents and abilities, personalities, and opportunities. What joy are you missing in life because you aren't using the capabilities and potentials you have been given? Jesus wants you to be your own person. Do you feel that someone else is more attractive than you are, more naturally intelligent or better proportioned physically? Are you using that as your excuse for not appreciating what you have been given? Because others have attributes you don't have is no basis for your feeling inferior or their feeling superior. First Corinthians 4:7 (*NIV*) puts it this way, "For who makes you different from anyone else? What do you have that you did not receive? And if you did receive it, why do you boast as though you did not?"

All of our natural abilities have come from the hand of a loving God. What matters now is our faithfulness in developing what God has given us, rather than arguing with God about what we don't have or wish we had. The time has come to accept what we've been given. We can then be excited and not threatened when someone else excels.

Have you ever taken a child out to a restaurant with you? You were probably excited about sharing the eating experience with her only to discover that she is upset because she doesn't have a straw! In front of her is a plate of delicious, attractively displayed food. But the only thing that matters is the missing straw!

How do you feel as a parent? Is it just possible we use similar antics when we focus on our deficits, compare them to other people's natural abilities and moan? There's a fabulously exciting world out there waiting to be explored and loved. Yet here we sit in our disbelief, eyes focused on ourselves, comparing ourselves with others and drowning in a pool of self-pity. It's time to refuse to feel second-rate because we are not perfect.

When we begin with what we have, as opposed to

what we don't have, we are often surprised at how very much God has given us with which to work. Take out a pen and paper and take some time to focus on your uniqueness.

1. Make a list of at least 10 things you like about yourself . . . 20 things would be even better. No doubt the Lord has brought special people into your life who have helped you develop these characteristics and have affirmed your growth along the way. Put their names down beside your list.

2. Spend time in prayer. Thank God for the 20 things you like about yourself. Do you realize you are praising God for His creation when you do this? Then thank God for the wonderful, affirming people He has brought into your life. Finally, thank God for creating you.

3. Next, make a list of the things you honestly don't like about yourself. Go back and put a checkmark beside the things you *could* change if it was important to you. Please keep this list. We will refer to it later in the book.

4. The unchecked items on your list are the things about yourself which you cannot change. The time has come to thank the Lord for these and to verbalize to Him your acceptance of this "thorn in your flesh." Write out an acceptance prayer to the Lord.

5. After you have written out your prayer of

acceptance, covenant with the Lord not to
ever again bemoan the areas you are incapable of changing.

God is limitless but we definitely are not. By working
through this exercise you choose the limitations you cannot change. You have also accepted them. This is a crucial
step on your spiritual journey. Let's not waste any more
time asking, "what if." If the limits on our ability can't be
changed, let's accept them and accept ourselves as God
does.

Joni Eareckson Tada has had to come to grips with the
reality that she is a quadraplegic. But that doesn't stop her
from ministering in word and song, from being an artist,
from writing or from encouraging others. Michelle Price
came face-to-face with the reality of cancer and had to
have a leg amputated. But that hasn't stopped her from
competing in winter sports.[2] What is the reality you have
just faced by writing out your prayer and covenant? That is
part of the beauty of you! Celebrate your uniqueness!

Enjoy the Trip

In this chapter we have begun the process of moving
towards interdependence by facing the question "How can
I love myself?" The process is far from complete but
since, "a journey of a thousand miles begins with a single
step," we have taken our first five steps. This is not a
magical journey. You will not wake up one morning and find
you have arrived at your destination. Rather, you will discover you were put on the face of this earth to enjoy the
trip. Serendipities await you. So take time to meditate on,
pray over and incorporate these into your life-style. In the
next chapter the process of learning to love ourselves, as
God loves us, will be continued.

6

Will I See a Difference in Myself?

Questioning Your Motivation

Based on a comprehensive view of Scripture, a woman who is growing toward interdependence believes three things: (1) she is highly significant to God; (2) she is deeply fallen; (3) she is greatly loved. This doesn't mean she simply gives intellectual assent to these truths. She has experienced these truths in the depth of her being.

How Do I Respond to My Mistakes?

I have found a good way to determine whether I have really grasped the reality of God's love for me and belief in me is to look at the way I handle my limitations, my mistakes and my failures. There are three questions I need to ask myself whenever I make a mistake:

1. *Do I make negative value judgments about myself based on my deficiency of my mistakes?*

   Does my self talk say, *I don't know how to play the piano.* Or does it say, *I'm worthless. I'm a flop. Everybody must think I'm a real dummy, a failure.*

2. *Do I run away from my deficiencies and mistakes?*

   Do I pretend the mistakes aren't there?

   Do I put on yet another mask?

   Do I blame my mistakes on other people or circumstances?

   Do I blame God?

   Am I once again running away from anyone or anything that makes me feel bad?

3. *Can I look at my deficiencies and own them without threat?*

   Can I forgive myself of my mistakes as God forgives me?

   Do I realize it is impossible to change lifetime habits overnight?

   Do I refuse to discriminate against myself?

None of us is strong or superior in everything. We are all inferior in some respect. I have always chuckled at Maxwell Maltz's statement that "nine-five percent of us suffer from feelings of inferiority and the other five percent are liars." It's true, so why do we forget so quickly? If we find ourselves answering the questions above by choosing either the first or second option, we must ask ourselves another question: *Do I want to believe what God says about me or would I rather suffer?*

Why Do I Choose Negativity?

It seems to me there can be a perverse sense of satisfaction in being negative about ourselves. There is even a security in it because if we are negative we only define what we are not. We don't ever have to define who we are. We say things like this:

"I'm such a failure."
"I can't do anything."
"There is no hope for me."
"I have no talent."
"My nose is too big" . . . and more.

After reading this list of negatives I want to ask you two questions: Are you any closer to knowing this woman (you!) who says such things about herself? Is she any closer to understanding herself? A resounding no is, of course, the answer to both questions. As a matter of fact, by constantly putting themselves down, many women chose the pathway to withdrawal. They hide behind the smoke screen of inferior feelings rather than face the truth that they don't really know themselves.

This doesn't mean we are never to experience negative thoughts and feelings about ourselves. That belief would make us phonies. Negative thoughts only indicate we are aware of our limitations. It is at that point we can work to change those limitations into areas of strength, if we consider them important enough.

If I want to be able to look at my deficiencies and own

Questioning Your Motivation

	Dependent	Independent	Interdependent
View of God	Afraid of the all powerful God who will punish me if I fail. Deeply spiritual and loves God greatly.	Ignores God. Doesn't need Him. "The sacred exists within me."	Awe and love. God is Holy. God is my friend. He wants what is best for me.
Motivation	Duty, guilt, fear, laziness or a desire to please.	Self.	Love.
Identity found	Through another person.	Ourselves.	Loving God, self and others.
Basic outlook	Negative. Sees problems. Carries crosses. Attempts to earn God's favor.	Fluctuates. If successful— positive. If failure— negative and angry.	Positive. Seizes opportunities. Faces challenges.
View of myself	Negative.	Inflated: "I am all that I need."	Positive. Sees myself as: a. highly significant; b. deeply fallen; c. greatly loved. "God is at work in me."

	Dependent	Independent	Interdependent
	See myself as not living up to "my" standards or "God's" standards. Punitive— condemning of self.		Sees possibilities. Can laugh at self. High self-esteem.
	Insecure, low or no self-esteem.		
View of others	Addictive relationships; needs others. Dependent on others.	Self-centered relationships. Uses others. Independence stemming from dependence.	Love relationships. Loves others. Dependent on God.
	Life revolves around others. Pushes for uniformity.	Life revolves around self.	Free to serve others. Balanced.
	Finds it difficult to forgive others.	Push for diversity. Finds it difficult to forgive others.	Pushes for unity and reconciliation. "I have been forgiven, therefore I can forgive."
	Ministers from a position of superiority— shares only when victorious.	Why minister? "You do your thing and I'll do mine."	Free to be vulnerable. Ministers out of love. Shares with you as a sister.
	Feelings of dread or panic at the thought of losing the people she depends on.	Doesn't get tied into relationships where she could be hurt.	Feelings of deep sadness when a relationship ends.

them as my own without threat, if I want to be able to release the hold my mistakes have on me, I must first believe what God has said about me. I must see myself as highly significant, deeply fallen and greatly loved.

One Sunday morning, Dr. Robert Schuller used this illustration. An artist asked a beggar if he could paint the beggar's picture. For lack of something to do, the beggar agreed. A few hours later the artist finished the painting and let the beggar look at it. Astonishment registered all over the beggar's face as he viewed the canvas.

"Who's that?" he asked, for before him was a painting of a tall, dignified gentleman.

The artist's reply came quietly back, "That's the you I see."

"Then" said the beggar, "that's the me I'll be." Jesus sees us, dear women, not as the sinner we indeed *are* but as the saint we *will be*.

If you ask this loving God to illuminate your life and believe what He has said about you, you are going to see some real changes in your outlook on life.

Look now at the comparison chart which illustrates the difference between the dependent woman who is motivated by guilt, the independent woman who is motivated by self and the interdependent woman whose motivation comes from love. Motivation is indeed everything!

What Do I Believe About God?

What a difference our thoughts and beliefs about God make. What is more security-producing than to know that the Creator of the universe is acquainted with me personally? He values me, understands me, infuses me with His life, acccepts me and loves me enough that He would allow His son to die in my place. What freedom comes with the realization that this same God has the power and desire to redeem all the experiences of my life. He longs to fill my emptiness with Himself and He is preparing a place for me in eternity where there will be no feelings of inferiority, no limitations. Philips Brooks has been quoted as saying: "The true way to be humble is not to stoop until you are smaller than yourself, but to stand at your real height against some higher nature that will show you what the real smallness of your greatness is."

The interdependent woman is the only woman who can stand tall and give life all she's got because her God is so much greater. She stands in awe of the love and beauty of God's plan. She is both truly humble and enthusiastically proud that she can have a part in touching a hurting world with God's love.

Unlike the dependent woman, she does not try to create herself into a loving person because that is what is expected of her. She can stop the straining, the super-woman antics, she can trust that since she has given Him the go-ahead, the Holy Spirit is creating God's "agape" love within her. She is indeed becoming a loving person.

Now instead of having her daily devotions so she can alleviate the pangs of guilt with which she is struggling, the interdependent woman realizes her need to be in Scripture so she can cooperate with God in this loving process. Instead of trying to pray a few seconds before she falls off to sleep, because if she doesn't she will feel guilty, prayer now becomes an affirmation of her openness to being changed. Prayer becomes an opportunity to receive Christ's power before she acts.

Prayer is often used to ask God's approval of our plans and to advance our causes. But because the interdependent woman understands God's love for her and His desire for her best, the cause she wants advanced is Christ's, even if that involves a change in her perspective.

Why Are My Relationships the Way They Are?

Dependent Relationships

Sometimes the change in perspective that takes place is almost overwhelming. In no area is this more evident than in our relationships with others. The dependent woman specializes in addictive relationships, for she has lost all sense of wholeness. She needs others and depends on them to determine her sense of self; she has no idea of who she is apart from them. Her life revolves around others and her hold on others could be described as a stranglehold. In the Body of Christ she pushes for "cookie cutter" Christians—for uniformity. If everyone looks the same way, believes the same things and does the same thing, she feels secure.

Often it is the dependent tendency in us which makes us set ourselves up as judges, to see if other people live up to *our* version of the scriptural standard. When people fail in her eyes, the dependent woman finds it very hard to forgive them. After all, she has never learned to forgive herself. The dependent woman may become aloof and withdrawn because she doesn't want you to be aware there are struggles in her life. When she does share with you, *if* she does, she will share with you from a position of superiority. It is only when she is experiencing victory that she will be open.

Independent Relationships

Antagonized by the dependent woman, the independent woman sets out to do her own thing. Yet I see the independent woman as dependent on others. She is just like the adolescent who is in rebellion against her parents as a matter of principle. She has to know what her parents' stand is on every issue so she can take the opposite position. That adolescent is not free! She is still dependent on her parents and tied to them, even though she believes she is independent. So it is with the dependent woman.

I discovered a column in a woman's magazine today called "Swap the Old Lady for a New Woman." The old lady column (a derogatory view of old, by the way) stresses dependence while the new lady column stresses independence. It seems to me the independent woman is reacting to the dependent woman, who she either used to be or is terrified of becoming. She does not want to have to live up to anyone's expectations but her own, so she pursues self-centered relationships. If you can meet some of her needs you will be her friend. If not, she doesn't have time for you.

There is one basic problem with such a self-centered existence. When we build our lives around ourselves and insist on filling all of our own needs, we find ourselves bound by the smallness of our lives. A sense of superiority is often a cover for feelings of inferiority. Instead of knocking herself down and condemning herself as the dependent woman might, the independent woman builds herself up. Oftentimes she knocks other people down in the process—be they women or men—to gain her sense of selfhood.

Interdependent Relationships

There is no freedom in either dependency or independence. We need to be a new creation, a woman who is not afraid of losing her identity if she loves. Walter Tubbs answers the *Gestalt Prayer*, mentioned in chapter two, and in the process defines the meaning of interdependence:

If I just do my thing and you do yours,
We stand in danger of losing each other and our-
    selves.

I am not in this world to live up to your expecta-
    tions;
But I am in this world to confirm you
As a unique human being
And to be confirmed by you.

We are fully ourselves only in relation to each
    other;
The I detached from a Thou
Disintegrates.

I do not find you by chance;
I find you by an active life of reaching out.
Rather than passively letting things happen to
    me,
I can act intentionally to make them happen.

I must begin with myself, true;
But I must not end with myself:
The truth begins with two.[1]

Only the interdependent woman achieves the balance
of freedom to be with others without being inhibited or
restricted by those relationships. This is the woman who
is free to be a wife and mother because her identity is not
found in the labels she wears. She is free to love and she is
free to serve, not out of duty but out of loving concern.

The interdependent woman pushes not for uniformity
but for unity and reconciliation. She realizes her personal
responsibility to be all she can be but she does not take it

upon herself to make you into her image. One of her goals in her relationships is to be the first one to make positive, concrete steps towards reconciliation whenever necessary. Because she realizes she is "in process" she makes an effort to view other people as in process also. A realization of how much Jesus Christ has forgiven her helps her when she is tempted to be judgmental and unforgiving.

This is the woman who wants you to be aware of her loving heavenly Father. Therefore she is free to share even in her weakness and need so you will be aware of God's creative activity in her life. She has nothing to prove to you, for she is secure in the love, acceptance and forgiveness offered to her by a loving God. She is able to let God love her and is free to be a loving human being.

Motivation Is Everything!

Indeed, our motivation makes an astounding difference. The dependent woman, bound as she is by guilt, duty and fear, faces life negatively. She is frustrated with God, herself and others most of the time. She seems to continually carry what she refers to as a cross. Because of her motivation, she sees problems when she looks at life.

By contrast, the independent woman's outlook on life is a fluctuating one. When she feels successful in achieving her personal goals she is positively inclined, but when she does not realize those goals she becomes negative and angry. You might even find yourself being blamed for her inability to reach her goal.

It is only the interdependent woman whose basic outlook on life can be positive. This is the woman who, when faced with problems, seizes opportunities to love and faces challenges head-on because Christ is her helper and guide. Instead of life becoming a condition for approval, this woman's life becomes a song of praise.

7

Why Again, Lord?

Dealing with Your Past

Why Look Back?

Proverbs 23:7 states that "As a [man] thinketh in his heart, so is he." I say, "As a woman thinketh so is she!" We act on the basis of our belief system and the truth of this statement makes it necessary for us to not only examine our beliefs but also the origins of our belief system. Even though we are not solely the product of our past it is a necessary first step, in becoming interdependent, to examine whether our thought patterns about ourselves are based on hearsay, from parents and peers, or on reality, as we see it.

Do you question the necessity of facing the past? Is it painful? The first major reason why healing memories is a necessity is because we aren't free to love others in our *present* when we're carrying so many scars from the *past*. How often do we run into people who remind us of people in our past who have hurt us?

The second marvelous reason for facing the past involves the emotional release one experiences when facing and forgiving. In Scripture we read that the truth sets us free. Let us go on record by saying the truth about ourselves can make us miserable. Only when it is confessed and forgiven are we set free. For years many of us have barricaded a part of ourselves and have refused to let God's love reach inside. What freedom comes to us when we do what we most fear and face our pain. We find a loving Saviour who is eager to hear our willingness to forgive as well as "cast our sins into the depth of the sea" (see Mic. 7:19).

A third amazing thing happens. When we forgive someone who has hurt us deeply, *they* seem to experience a new freedom. One can only imagine what would have happened in young Saul's life if Stephen hadn't uttered these words to the Lord as he was being stoned to death: "Lord, do not hold this sin again them" (Acts 7:60). This was, beyond a doubt, one of the tools used by the Holy Spirit as He transformed young, intelligent, well-bred Saul into the Apostle Paul. *Am I blocking a freedom the Holy Spirit desires someone to have?*

The Lord has made *our* forgiveness dependent on our willingness to forgive, even if no one has asked us, and this is the last reason we need to face our past. Mark 11:25-26 *(NASB)* states it clearly: "And whenever you stand praying, forgive, if you have anything against anyone; so that your Father also who is in heaven may forgive you your transgressions. But if you do not forgive, neither will your Father who is in heaven forgive your transgressions."

It is a well-known fact that we act not on the basis of reality but on the basis of our perception of reality. I may see an attractive middle-aged woman approaching me on the street. You also see her and based on the warm, accepting relationships you have experienced in your past with women of this age group, you will find yourself anticipating meeting this stranger. On the other hand, if I have felt rejection from my mother, from my aunt or from a middle-aged teacher in my past, I might be extraordinarily leery of coming face-to-face with her. Our past affects our perception of the present.

As a child we learn who we are and who we are not from the people around us. This doesn't change as we mature. A teenager's peer group is extremely important to their search for identity. As an adult we choose the people we have around us and that group will also be an extremely important indicator of who we are. What we believe others think of us is crucial to our feelings and understanding of ourselves.

Where did those negative feelings you have about yourself originate? When did your negative self-talk originate? Where did your fear of leaving the familiar, your lack of direction in your life and your frustration with your limitations come from? Facing our discontent is necessary to the healing of our many childhood memories.

It is also necessary to establish, before we begin to recall our childhood, that the purpose of this exercise is not to tear our parents apart limb by limb. They did the best they could do given the emotional, spiritual and financial resources they had at the time. The purpose of taking the time to remember is to discover where our positive and negative ideas about ourselves have come from. Perhaps we will also unearth how our concept of God has evolved, since many of us have difficulty understanding God as Father because of painful relationships we have experienced with our earthly fathers. Lastly, this journey backwards will give us new insights into the relationship or lack of relationship our parents shared. Many of us, even today, are affected by that relationship which seemed so very normal to us for so long.

Be Real About Your Past

What do you remember about your life between the ages of birth to five years? Six years to 10? 11 years to 14? 15 years to 20? Take the time to get comfortable and to really let your mind wander into your past. Perhaps you will find it helpful to play some soft orchestration, to close your eyes and be still. Ask your heavenly Father to take this journey backwards with you and ask the Holy Spirit to bring those memories to your mind which will aid you in your understanding of why you feel the way you do about yourself.

Remembering Family Relationships

Do you remember much about your parents? How would you describe your mother—your father—your sisters—your brothers? What kind of a relationship did you have with your sisters or brothers? How would you describe your relationship with your parents? What upset your parents about you and how did they express their frustration to you? What feelings did you pick up from them about the way you looked—about the accomplishments you made at school? How were you compared to your brothers and sisters? Were your feelings accepted and considered by your parents or did you grow up learning to distrust your own feelings?

Your Parents and Their God

Did your father have a personal relationship with Jesus Christ? How would you describe this relationship? How do you think your father viewed God? Did your father ever discuss his faith with you? What was your emotional reaction to these discussions? Did your mother have a personal relationship with Jesus Christ? How would you describe this relationship? How do you think your mother viewed God? Did your mother ever discuss her faith with you? What was your emotional reactions to these discussions?

Your Parents' Relationship

How did your family view relationships with other people? Would you say your family put a greater emphasis on relationships or accomplishments? Did you feel valued by your parents? Did you feel your parents valued each other? What was your mother's style of relating to others—dependent, independent or interdependent? What was your father's style of relating to others—dependent, independent or interdependent? What feelings did you pick up about the concept of submission?

Your Parents and You

What did you have to do to win your parents' approval? How did they express their approval and disapproval of you? Do you feel close to both of your parents? Do you feel closer to your mother or to your father? Are you similar to your mother? In what ways are you similar to your father? How are you different from your mother? How are you different from your father? What do you appreciate most about your mother? What do you appreciate most about your father? How did your parents handle your developing sexuality? How did they deal with your steps toward independence? What was their attitude about your leaving the nest? Are your growing up years a joyful experience to remember or have these questions stirred up emotions of sadness, despair, bitterness, anger or even hate?

Acknowledging the Wounded Child

Just this past week I came in contact with a beautiful young woman. Maria was adopted as a child and throughout her 28 years of life has been carrying around deep feelings of rejection. Maria cannot understand the desire her adoptive parents had for her, the heartache they felt as the legalities increased their time of waiting, the sacrifice they made financially to get her and the fear they experienced until they knew she was really going to be allowed to stay in their family. Her vision is clouded and she cannot focus on how very much she was wanted. Rejection is all she can see. Her new husband is doing all he can to fill her need for acceptance, as did her adoptive family before him, but to no avail. Maria is continually searching for acceptance. She wants to be held on an extremely high pedestal and worshiped, as it were, to prove that she is acceptable. In fact, this need is making her a prime candidate for an affair. Why is all of this happening to such a beautiful, competent woman? It is occurring because there is a rejected and deeply-wounded child inside the very competent adult Maria—a child who is certain no one really wants her.

Are you carrying a deeply wounded little child within you? If you are, this child will affect every area of your life. It will affect whether you choose marriage or singleness. It will affect your career, your friendships, your attitudes, your capacity to change, your actions and reactions, your values, your happiness (or lack of it) and finally, your style of relating to God, yourself and others.

Perhaps as a child your parents mirrored non-acceptance to you. Perhaps your grades were the issue, your athletic ability or just your overall prowess. Perhaps you constantly found yourself being compared to your sister and you felt like the bottom of a totem pole. It didn't take you long as a child to decide that you were not as good as other people. Then you took your negative value system into the cruel world. At school your peers were unmerciful, they labeled you "stupid" and this reinforced your fragile, negative belief system. You told yourself others felt the same way your parents did so therefore, the harsh criticism must be true. Somewhere along the line you decided to talk to yourself in this negative, derogatory way. It wasn't long before you believed that other people in the world, people you hadn't even met yet, felt the same way about you. They saw you as incompetent, too.

Does the Child Still Hurt?

If you now happen to attend a church which focuses heavily on your unworthiness, sin and guilt, you must constantly go away knowing nothing but condemnation and never experiencing the freedom Jesus wants to give you. The burden of this condemnation is so phenomenally overwhelming you decide to prove to the world that you *are* acceptable by being spunky, getting even or withdrawing behind a mask and eventually behind closed doors. Perhaps you've become the clown or little miss spirituality. Maybe you've lowered your standards to prove you were acceptable. Perhaps you've rejected your parents' lifestyle and joined a peer group where you found acceptance. Perhaps you choose to be so busy you don't have to think about the issue at all. Perhaps you've retreated behind a box of chocolates in front of the television set.

What happens when criticism comes from the people you're trying so hard to impress? Anywhere we find ourselves in the world, there will be criticism. We *all* fail and have to face our failures. But each time you are faced with a failure, is it proof positive, to your hurt inner child, that you are incapable, unacceptable and stupid? As your self-image becomes severely malformed by the blows life deals, do you reject even the positive pieces of information coming your way? How do you respond to a compliment? Can you say thank-you and accept it or are your uncomfortable when faced with affirmations?

If you are involved in a relationship, do you find yourself clinging to your very special person, afraid that he too is going to find out the truth about you, criticize you and abandon you? Do you find yourself smothering the life out of him? If you are in a position of power, do you find yourself giving in to the internal tendency to criticize and condemn others before they can do it to you? Do you come unglued when an employee finds fault with some facet of your business?

Where did this germ of self-hate, which has spread into a cancerous disease, come from? It began in so many of our pasts when we were severely and harshly criticized, compared, labelled and even abused.

Won't the Pain Go Away?

I can almost hear some of you precious readers now, sharing Paul's writing from Philippians 3:13-14 *(NASB)* with me: " . . . but one thing I do: forgetting what lies behind and reaching forward to what lies ahead. I press on toward the goal for the prize of the upward call of God in Christ Jesus." It seems to me that there is only one way to forget the past; we must deal with it. The past needs to be faced before it can be filed under "forgiven and reprogrammed." If we are full of fear, hate and prejudice, these will dictate our behavior. If we think we can just shove the past under the surface and walk away from it, one day we will find ourself in a new situation or in front of a stranger who will trigger a memory button. For no explainable reason we might find ourselves intensely disliking the stranger or dealing with a surge of negative emotions that threaten to overwhelm us. If we assume the ostrich stance with our head in the sand, ignoring the past, we are limiting the healing the Holy Spirit so desires to bring into our lives. The past must be dealt with before we can begin to love ourselves, our God and our neighbors. Proverbs bears repeating, "As a [woman] thinketh in her heart so is [she]." Denis Waitley puts it this way:

All individuals are born without a sense of self. We are like tape recorders without the key message—with some prerecorded facts and background music, but no central theme. We are like mirrors with no reflections. First through our senses, during infancy—then through language and observation—we tape record, build and photograph our video, audio and sensory cassettes of ourselves. This recorded self-concept or self-image—this mental picture of self—when nourished and cultivated, is a primary field in which happiness and success grow and flourish. But this same mental self-concept, when undernourished or neglected, becomes a spawning pond for low achievement, defiant behavior, and unhappiness.[1]

Yanking Out Your Elephant Stake

As a child I remember sitting in church when my father told this story of an elephant. Did you know that an adult elephant, weighing 10 tons, can be tied to the same size stake that a 300-pound baby elephant is tied to and never pull it out? When the large elephant was a baby he was secured by this stake. Try as he might, he found it impossible to escape. For the rest of his life, even as a 10-ton elephant, the animal remembers he cannot get away from that stake.

Are we a little like that elephant? Did someone in our past tell us we weren't pretty, we wouldn't amount to much or we were stupid? When did we start believing them? When did we drive an elephant stake into our subconscious mind? As adult women, are we being held back by some erroneous stake from our past?

My sixth grade teacher, who also happened to be my first male instructor, told me (no doubt in desperation) in a physical education class one day that I was the clumsiest person he had ever seen. That comment hurt and it has stuck with me all these years. To this day when I walk in front of a group, especially of men, that stake wants to hold me down. I was also the adolescent with the purple acne. It cleared up long ago but when a pimple appears now it is easy to overreact and recall those adolescent feelings. A dear friend who has lost a great deal of weight shared with me the other day that her inner tape needs to be reprogrammed because it is very easy for her to still feel tremendously overweight. What inaccurate tape is playing in your mind? What "elephant stakes" have you driven deep in your subconscious? Do you desire to be healed, to cooperate with the spirit of our Lord by pulling the stakes out? Or do you want to continue the pattern you have established?

Deal with Your Past

If the ache is excruciating enough, the pain so intense that you desire the Holy Spirit's healing touch on your memories, there are five steps you must first take to deal effectively with your past.

1. Invite the Holy Spirit to Take Part in Your Journey

This is not a journey for us to embark on alone. This is not to be a solo flight. For this voyage we need to be dependent on our Lord and on His Holy Spirit. But this same Spirit needs a personal invitation to take this journey with us. Never will God barge in and force Himself on us. He needs to be invited in. "Behold, I stand at the door and knock; if any one hears my voice and opens the door, I will come in to [her] and will dine with [her] and [she] with me" (Rev. 3:20, *RSV*). Every aspect of God is available to us all but we must extend the invitation, we must turn the tap on as it were. Imagine a narrow pipe coming straight down from heaven. This pipe carries all of God's grace, love, power and healing to each one of us. In the center of this pipe there is a tap. What power we have! By turning the tap off we can shut off the flow of God to us. We can go thirsty if we choose to. Or we can turn the knob and open up the pipe so all the power of God is available to each one of us. Our inner self is God's terrain but we must take an active part in the exploration of that newfound land.

By choosing to be an ostrich, by refusing to face our painful memories and our hurts, we have turned off the tap. We have refused to allow God's cooling waters of forgiveness and healing to touch our pain and we will continue to find ourselves parched, cracked, dry and oh, so thirsty. Let's lay down our reading for a moment and let's together invite the Holy Spirit to accompany us on our journey backwards. A written invitation is always a thrill to receive. Let's extend a written invitation to our precious Lord:

> Holy Spirit, today I invite you to walk down the corridors of my past with me. I ask you to bring to my mind incidents that have brought me pain, people who I would just as soon forget because they have hurt me or I have hurt them. Bring to my consciousness attitudes which are unhealthy and delusions under which I have been living. Today I turn on the tap so all of you can flow freely to all of my pain and need. Thank you for coming Holy Spirit. I don't want to stop the flow of your Spirit ever again.
>
> Signed,
>
> (Name)_____
>
> (Date)_____

Praise God! He is nearer to us than any problem, any conflict, any pain. Our Lord is in us and with us. The next helpful step after extending our written invitation to the Holy Spirit is—

2. Listen to Yourself.

What have our bodies been telling us lately? Our marvelously created bodies are in many ways alarm systems, designed to go off when things are not right. Have you found yourself overwhelmingly fatigued for no apparent reason? Have you been furiously angry and amazed at the depth of anger within your being? What about depression?

Do you find yourself depressed most of the time or do you only get depressed in certain situations. Are there roots of deep-seated negativity, jealousy, bitterness and competition within you? What have you been dreaming about lately? Would you classify yourself as healthy or have you been physically ill a great deal in the past few months? When was the last time you had a physical? What is your body saying to you? If we are to love ourselves we must learn to listen.

3. Face the Master Openly

When we make Jesus our Lord and Saviour we give this Redeemer our lives. With all His graciousness our Lord lovingly takes our gift and thanks us for it. We've given Jesus the gift of ourselves, or have we? Often what we've done is give the Lord the wrapping paper and the beautifully colored bow on our package. We've given Him a superficial gift.

Jesus desires that we get to know ourselves deeply and give Him whatever is real—not just the shiny, pretty, sweet-smelling, competent parts. Prior to making Jesus our Lord there is a lot of clutter, garbage and pain in our lives. Perhaps we have a prick of conscience periodically but that prick certainly fades away as the years pass. Then we invite this light of the world to be our Lord and suddenly all the garbage, clutter, pain that has been festering is exposed. Whatever is inside us is totally known to Jesus—the hurt, pain, anger, fear, whatever. He is never shocked by it. He is never repulsed by it. Why, that's what He died for. He came to this earth to redeem it. But what do we do? Often we slam the door on it, pretend it isn't there, act as if everything is fine and wonderful and assume the stance of an ostrich. Just like the ostrich, if it doesn't work well to put our head in the sand we will run faster than anyone else and get busier and busier. If we are hiding our hurt inner child from anyone, it certainly isn't God. Most likely we are hiding it from ourselves.

4. Drop Your Masks

Over and over again we hear committed Christian teachers tell us to do what is right even if the feelings aren't there and to act as if something is true and eventually the emotions will follow. Never would I deny the truth of this statement—but in the area of the healing memories it has to be applied very carefully. Taken to its extreme, this advice can lead us into acting spiritual while we're developing an ulcer as a result of our internal gymnastics. God is deeply concerned about our relationship with ourself. He wants those of us who are divided to be reconciled to Him *and* to ourselves. This is never accomplished by wearing a mask.

I love Paul's writings, for Paul was free to share himself with people. The more I read the epistles the more I become aware of his willingness to share his deep emotions with fellow believers. "For we do not want you to be ignorant, brethren, of the affliction we experienced in Asia; for we were so utterly, unbearably crushed that we despaired of life itself" (2 Cor. 1:8, *RSV*). Never does he set himself up as "Mr. Perfect" in order to help people. But sometimes we, as Christians, even use our faith as an excuse for failing to be honest with each other. Our logic goes something like this. "I'm a Christian now. I'm not supposed to be depressed or have an uncontrollable temper. I'm supposed to have overcome these things. I better not let others know what I'm really like or they won't think I'm much of a Christian." So we put on a mask and our pride gets entangled in the mask. We're phonies and we know it, but we must keep others from guessing the truth.

We end up lonely and cut off from others. The longer we pretend the deeper grows the gnawing fear that sometime we'll let the mask slip.

We are in need of a Saviour. After all, isn't that why we asked Jesus to be our Lord in the first place? It is only pride that tells us we must minister as the strong one to the weak. In reality we are called to minister as one needy human being to another needy human being. When we minister in this way others come away seeing the magnificence of our Lord. They desire Him, they praise Him and they see their need of Him rather than thinking, "I can't possibly be as good a Christian as she is." It's the difference between seeing grace or being faced with our inability to be perfect and leaving guilty and put down.

Pause right now and ask the Holy Spirit to make you aware of the masks you have been wearing. Spend some quiet time waiting on the Lord about this matter. As the masks and the phoniness are brought to your mind, confess and ask the Lord for His forgiveness. Confess that once again, you've tried to be the all-perfect one instead of letting God be the all knowing, all wise, holy, perfect, loving Father. Ask the Holy Spirit to make you aware the next time you start to hide behind another mask. Enjoy the healing as it comes straight from the hand of God. Be refreshed in Him! Praise and thank Him for His all encompassing forgiveness, acceptance and love.

5. Understand the Source of Your Pain

Questions have been provided throughout this chapter which I pray have been helpful to you in reviewing the stages of your past and in attempting to unearth any memories that still cause you pain. As that pain, which has been festering for years, is exposed to the Light it becomes evident that three things can be traced to the source. First,

*perhaps we locked the doors in our life because of sin—
something we have done or neglected to do.* Perhaps we
haven't used the gifts our Lord has given us for healing and
love. Perhaps they have only been used to build the kingdom of ourselves and the result has been pain.

Second, *it is also possible that our pain is caused by
something that someone has done to us.* This pain is the
result of another's sin against us. This pain can exist on
either a conscious level or on a subconscious level. I have
a dear friend who had a recurring problem which centered
around an inability to trust men. As she sought the Holy
Spirit's assistance in walking through her past, a picture
flashed into her mind of an uncle sexually molesting her.
Perhaps you were abused as a child or raped as an adult.
You especially know the excruciating pain of having someone sin against you. Perhaps you have been the victim of
withheld love. Others can cause us much pain and if it
hurts too much and we feel incapable of doing anything to
stop their sin against us, we often shove that hurt under
the surface and into our subconscious.

*Lastly, there may be festering sores in our emotional
lives because of something that has happened to someone else
we care deeply for.* We pick up someone else's pain and
carry it for them. But did you know that often, they're not
carrying it at all? To this day I find it easier to be criticized
myself, which still is not a lot of fun, than to hear my family
criticized, especially my husband. Perhaps this is an area
that we who have been or are pastors' wives are particularly susceptible. In our very first pastorate I had a lady
turn to me during the Sunday morning worship service
with these words, "Doesn't your husband have anything
else to wear? I'm so tired of seeing him in that one suit."
Believe me, this is a mild example of what happens to pastors' wives and children. But whatever the situation, perhaps there is pain in your life because you have been car-

rying someone else's pain all these years.

Now Let Him Heal Your Past

As women eager to be created into interdependent women by the Holy Spirit, there are six choices we need to be willing to make in order to find inner healing.

1. I Choose to Focus on God's Forgiveness and Acceptance of Me

> "I have wiped out your transgressions like a thick cloud, and your sins like a heavy mist. Return to Me, for I have redeemed you" (Isa. 44:22, *NASB*).

> "As far as the east is from the west, so far has He removed their transgressions from us" (Ps. 103:12, *NASB*).

> "And their sins and their lawless deeds I will remember no more" (Heb. 10:17, *NASB*).

Our God is never shocked. He knows the parts of us we aren't even aware of. Satan is the condemner, Jesus Christ is not. It would be extremely helpful to commit the above verses to memory. Meditate on them and get to know your Lord in a new way. Often I discover that God has accepted in me what I am having difficulty forgiving another person for. It is a worthwhile exercise to make a list of 10 things Christ has forgiven you for. Then write forgiven and accepted over your list. When you believe this you have really come to terms with how much God loves you. Then ask yourself, "Who has hurt me the very most." Retreat for a time of extended prayer to love that person with God's type of love.

I have found it helpful in my own life to hear a trusted friend speak Jesus' promise of forgiveness to me. We are just like Lazarus who when physically dead was raised to new life by Jesus' word. Even though he was to live, Lazarus had to be unbound by the hands of his close friends, who willingly took the grave clothes off of him and put up with the stench. In many ways we have been dead to a portion of our emotional self. We come to a new awareness of God's love, forgiveness and acceptance through Jesus' word. Then we find we need to be unbound by the hands of a close loving friend or by the hands of a trained Christian psychologist or pastor who is willing to face the garbage, the hurt, the pain with us and point us again to a forgiving Lord. We often feel God's forgiveness more when spoken in audible terms by the voice of a friend. It is one of the ways we can be God's voice to those around us.

2. I Choose to Change My Habit Pattern of Rehearsing Past Hurts

In the past, when we have experienced deep hurt, it is likely that we responded one of two ways. We either rehearsed the hurt so faithfully we hated the person who hurt us or we withdrew from the situation. Both responses are dangerous. In the first instance we end up being controlled by the person we are cursing. In the second case we have erased the possibility of a positive message overriding the hurt. We have closed out God's love and the human love that others want to give us. Let's change our habit pattern. Let's stop flogging others and flogging ourselves. Let's focus on God's forgiveness and acceptance of us. Let's stop waiting for some magical time when all of our unrealistic standards for ourselves and others have been met. Judas focused on his guilt and hung himself. Peter focused on our Lord's forgiveness and he hung up the guilt. Let's do likewise.

3. I Choose to Confess Immediately and to Forgive without Being Asked

I have found in my own life that confession must be immediate. The longer I nurse my hurt or rehearse my guilt, the harder it is to let it go. I keep a prayer journal and I find it extremely helpful to write out my prayers of confession. After them I often write the words of 1 John 1:9 *(NASB)*, "If we confess our sins, He is faithful and righteous to forgive us our sins and to cleanse us from all unrighteousness."

Since God's hands of forgiveness are tied until we are willing to forgive those who have hurt us, I choose to forgive. I do this because of my Lord's example. As I write this, Easter is one week away. I have been meditating on the day prior to and following Christ's death and resurrection. Christ was rejected by those into which He had poured His life and love. He was jeered and He was publicly humiliated. He was hung naked and exposed to the stares of men, women and children. He was hung between two common criminals. Not one of the jeering mob sought His pardon at Calvary. What was His response? He was willing to forgive people who had no comprehension of their need to be forgiven: "Father, forgive them for they know not what they do."

Peter once asked Christ how often he would need to forgive someone who had offended him. Jesus' reply was "as many as seven times seventy." On Calvary, the creator God of our universe lived out the truth of His words. We are often called to repeatedly forgive—especially after family gatherings held during the major holidays! I choose to forgive. I choose to obey. It's up to God to release my emotions. I will know I have been forgiven when I can face the cause of my pain and not feel turmoil.

4. I Choose to Be Dependent on God's Resources

Building the kingdom of "me" will not release the inner hurts and tapes of my past. My highest aim in life must be to know Christ. Often in this process we need to be willing to wait, the very thing many of us find most difficult. There are so many Scriptures referring to waiting.

> In repentance and rest you shall be saved, in quietness and trust is your strength (Isa. 30:15, *NASB*).

> Yet those who wait for the Lord will gain new strength; they will mount up with wings like eagles, they will run and not get tired, they will walk and not become weary (Isa. 40:31, *NASB*).

> I am the vine, you are the branches; he who abides in Me, and I in him, he bears much fruit; for apart from Me you can do nothing (John 15:5, *NASB*).

There is no shortcut to cooperating with God in changing ourselves. It involves waiting silently; it involves filling our minds with God's Word; it involves meditation.

When we try to love independently of God's resources we often do it to get something back, to manipulate or to impress. Let's ask God for the love and compassion we need to love ourselves and others.

5. I Choose to Love Unconditionally and Creatively the Person I Am Struggling Against

Jesus Christ offers us an unconditional, initiating love. How many times we put "ifs" on our loving. We tell ourselves that *if* she will do such and such *then* I will love her. God's love isn't dependent on what we do or what others do. Thank goodness! It's as if we have a giant magnifying glass within our heads; a glass that enlarges the negative in ourselves and others out of proportion. Our love isn't dependent on other people meeting our expectations. Our love is only dependent on God. Then in faith we act.

Have you thought of asking God for His creativity in loving someone you've been struggling against? Have you asked God to help you see that precious person through His eyes? Sometimes it is necessary to provide a time when we can mourn the relationship we never had. After we have worked through that process, with the Holy Spirit's guidance, it is easier to go on with reality-based expectations concerning that person.

There is a person in my life whom I have mourned. She is incapable of giving me the type of relationship I desire. This relationship has taught me many valuable lessons, including one on love: you learn to love by giving away *all* you have to give. In prayer one day the Holy Spirit convinced me that I needed to make it a point of doing one affirming thing for my friend each week, even while I was going through this mourning process. It's been fascinating to watch the relationship slowly, oh so slowly, take a turn for the better. A real moment of truth came when I received my contract for this book. Guess who I shared the good news with? That's right! I chose to unconditionally and creatively love the person I had been struggling against and the Holy Spirit did a loving work in me.

6. I Choose to Be Grateful for the Growth Resulting from the Hurt

At this stage we choose to ask ourselves, *How can I grow from this pain?* rather than using the condemning words, *I should have.* This is the time when we pray, *Lord help me to learn positive lessons from the hurtful things I will encounter in life* rather than praying, *Lord, don't let me be hurt anymore.* In our world it takes people who have experienced and worked through pain to be able to minister. These women will be less likely to throw out pat, unthinking answers. They will be less likely to clout you over the head with Scripture verses. They will be less likely to be Job's comforters. They will listen, love and lead you to the resources of the Lord Jesus Christ.

The choices we make enable us, with the Holy Spirit's guidance, to reprogram our thoughts and our habits when reacting against anyone or anything that hurts us. As women moving toward interdependence, we have valuable choices when dealing with pools of pain in our lives. The first step towards interdependence is a step backwards. It opens the locked doors of our lives where we have not felt the warmth of Jesus' accepting and forgiving love for years. How warm the Son feels!

8

Do I Have to Be All Things to All People

Beating the Superwoman Myth

Interdependent women are continually in process and I choose the word "process" because it points out an important truth—we will never arrive. When you were a child perhaps you collected butterflies and made a display plaque onto which they were mounted. Interdependence isn't like that. We can't collect it. We can only celebrate it.

Our individual process begins with a personal relationship with Jesus Christ. Because of Calvary He gives each of us the opportunity to view ourselves as a highly valuable person. It then becomes necessary to balance the acceptance of our humanity, and the needs and limitations that come with it, with our affirmation that we are first-class quality. Trying harder, as the superwoman does, will never change us into deity.

The superwoman spends every waking moment comparing herself with a fantasy. She compares everyone else's best with her worst. She pressures herself with a vision of perfection. She cannot, of course, live up to the expectations she has set for herself but she feels like a total failure anyway. In fact, if she continues she is well on her way to being a *totalled* woman.

Pull Out of the Competition

How do we grow as Christian women? Certainly not through competition. Do you find yourself involved in activities in which you are competing with those around you? Do you feel a pressure to be a superwoman? Perhaps it would be wise to consider pulling away and using the time to evaluate and focus on what God wants to do in your life.

The Christian woman has been freed from the necessity to compete. Her assignment is to cooperate with the Holy Spirit and what He wants to do in her life. So this becomes the key question:

Am I willing to embark on a joint adventure with the Holy Spirit?

In Philippians 2:12-13 *(RSV)* we read, "work out your own salvation with fear and trembling; for God is at work in you, both to will and to work for his good pleasure."

This doesn't mean we can save ourselves or can work our way into a right relationship with God by our own efforts. If this were possible it would be most appealing to the independent superwoman in each one of us. It does mean we are to join God in working out those things He is most effectively working on. Our assignment is to cooperate with the Holy Spirit and there are three very practical ways we can do this.

Be in the Word (see 1 Tim. 2:15)

Why? Not for the reason *I* used to read Scripture, which was to alleviate my feelings of guilt. You see, I knew it was something I was supposed to do if I was going to be a good Christian, so most nights I mechanically read a few verses, wondering all the while why so many people made so much of it. Personally, I found it quite a bore.

It wasn't until my guilt-motivation was replaced by a love-motivation that I discovered I *wanted* to be in cooperation with this Saviour who loved me so very much. I wanted to learn more about this holy, loving, forgiving, accepting Lord so when my mind was centered on Him, the Holy Spirit would transform me into a loving, forgiving, accepting person.

We must be in the Word so we can discover where we need to grow to achieve our full potential. Just as electricity must run through a conductor, so must the Holy Spirit work through the means God has provided—His Word. Have you asked the Lord to make you enthusiastic about meeting with Him daily? It's a daily battle for all of us, isn't it! Just as we don't get food for our bodies by looking at the unopened packages in our pantry, neither do we get spiritual food from an unopened Bible. We can attend three Bible studies a week, two seminars a month, all the church services available to us and hear others talk about the Word, but it won't nourish our spirits unless we personally take in the Word of God on a regular basis. We are limiting what the Holy Spirit can do in our lives otherwise.

The story is told of a husband whose wife died suddenly. He was left alone and broken to father their precious little girl. When the first Christmas holiday arrived he decided to take the week off and spend it with his daughter. How he was anticipating that shared time. When the first morning finally came the father rose excitedly, only to find that his daughter had shut herself in her room and would not come out until suppertime. The distraught father didn't know what to do.

Finally Christmas morning arrived and under the tree was a package wrapped in newspaper, tape and layers of ribbons. Triumphantly the little girl offered it to her beloved daddy. Upon opening it he discovered a pair of socks she had knitted for him. "Daddy, this is what I was working on each day for you!" she exclaimed. The daddy gathered her up in his arms, hugged her and with tears rolling down his cheeks said, "Honey, I love the socks, they're beautiful. But all I wanted was time with you."

I wonder how often Jesus weeps over our busyness, our independence, our service for Him—longing to say to us. "My child, I just want time with you." Moffatt's translation of Isaiah 65:1 goes like this: "Ready was I to answer [women] who never . . . sought me. I cried out, 'Here am I,' to folk who never called to me."

Pause now and spend a moment centering all your thoughts on Jesus. Talk to Him about your desire to know Him better. Now ask Him to make you enthusiastic about time alone with Him. He desires time with you, not to make you feel guilty, but rather so He can love you into your full potential as an interdependent woman. But beware. It could be habit forming!

Be in Prayer (see 1 Thess. 5:17)

The duty-motivated person reads this suggestion for cooperating with the Holy Spirit and asks, "Haven't you laid enough guilt trips on us?" After all, when we're guilt-motivated we *do* pray. But we often ask God to put His okay on our plans and causes just before we fall into bed at night, exhausted. Then we fall off to sleep, relieved that we've done our duty.

The woman who is deeply touched by God's love for her prays because she is open to being changed. She admits her need for Christ's power to act. She prays in order to get a new perspective and to advance the cause of Jesus Christ.

We are in an exhilarating, creative partnership with the God of the universe when we pray. Prayer is not just a one-way communication with God where we tell Him all our needs and problems. It is also a time to adore, confess and thank our loving heavenly Father. It is a time to be completely honest with God. Are you angry with God? Confess it! He won't faint. He knows it already. Prayer is a time to ask questions and wait for His ideas and answers.

It is also a time to be silent and to open your mind so God's thoughts will flow in to you. The psalmist writes,

> Make me know Thy ways, O Lord;
> Teach me Thy paths.
> Lead me in Thy truth and teach me,
> For Thou art the God of my salvation;
> For Thee I wait all the day. (Ps. 25:4-5 *NASB*).

God wants to shape our will and direct our steps. He will enlarge our vision through prayer and give each of us a dream which would be impossible without Him. Prayer will open up new possibilities in our world. Anne Ortlund uses an illustration comparing life to a funnel. The non-Christian woman enters at the wide end and finds that as she progresses through life, her options are narrowed until she finally finds herself at a deadend with no hope in sight. By contrast the Christian woman enters at the narrow end of the funnel, through belief in Jesus Christ as her Saviour, and then finds all of life in its fullness opening up to her as she travels on through.

Do you feel a need to enlarge your vision or to change your perspective? Then cultivate your prayer life. Dream

God's dreams for your life and your situation.

Be Your Own Best Friend (see Mark 12:31)

One of the cruelest things we can possibly do to another person is to withdraw our hope from them. Is it possible you have done this to yourself? What kind of an opinion do you have of yourself? Do you look for the best in yourself?

There isn't any opinion more important to your well-being than the opinion you hold of yourself. Do you treat yourself as if you were a beloved friend? In the last week, what did you do just for yourself? I'm aware that as a woman you are probably called on to do many things for others, but what have you done for yourself? Have you even allowed yourself the joy of stopping and smelling the flowers?

It doesn't glorify God when you nag one of God's children. Remember, you are one of God's precious children! How have you been talking to yourself? Some people are cursed with a computer in their brain, programmed to find the worst in everything and everyone, including themselves. Are you one of these people?

One word of destructive self-criticism does about 10 times as much damage to your self-esteem as a word of criticism from someone else.[1] Women who verbally downgrade themselves with consistency will eventually come to the point of believing what they hear. Once they believe, they automatically act on their beliefs.

It becomes obvious then, that our words program our spirit either to success or defeat. How do you talk to yourself? How do you talk about yourself? Do you build your own set of limitations by the words you say? Are your words faith words or slave words? Does your vocabulary consist more of "I can," "I choose," "I will" or "I'm not,"

"I can't" and "I won't." One of the surest ways to lose our sense of self-worth is by persecuting ourselves with unreasonable, unscriptural, illogical and negative thoughts.

Years ago, my husband and I house sat for a couple who were often called away on weekend business trips. Five high school through college-age boys came with the house! We'd move in, cook the meals, attempt to keep the schedules straight and try to maintain order. How indebted we are for the lessons we learned from that wonderful family. One of the best lessons was the "no knock" policy in their home. Criticism of other people or of one another was not tolerated at a meal or any other time.

Isn't it time we adopt the no knock policy for ourselves? What do we gain through criticizing ourselves? We gain a self-centered perspective, we adopt no personal responsibility for change and we fill ourselves full-to-over-flowing with self-pity. Is that what the Holy Spirit desires for us? It's almost as if we're tempting God by saying, "I dare you to do anything with this negative, depressed and discouraged lump of humanity."

Philippians 4:8 tells us to *dwell* on things that are true, honorable, right, pure, lovely, excellent and of good report. Are these the things on which you have been dwelling? In John 10:10 we learn that it is Satan's purpose to steal, kill, destroy and tear down. Whose side are you on? Have you been cooperating with the Holy Spirit or with the devil?

From this point on let's make it a habit to affirm ourselves. Let's be sure that our self-talk is consistent with God's Word. Now stop for a moment and repeat these statements out loud:

"I am highly significant to God."
"I am of great value to God."

"I am loved by God."
"I am unique."
"I am special."
"I'm glad that I am me."
"I'm glad I am alive."
"I am glad I am a woman."
"I am glad I am single/married."
"I am God's precious child."
"I am a loving and gentle person."
"I am a joyful person."
"I am a patient person."
"I am a trustworthy friend."
"I am a thankful person."

Add some of your own affirmations to this list.

Saying words like these is like watering seeds. Don't underestimate the power of positive affirmations.

Follow Christ's example by prayerfully exchanging your negative names for yourself with positive ones. This isn't looking at the world through rose-colored glasses. This is faith! Giving yourself a positive, scriptural affirmation will also be one of the best ways of fighting off those superwoman tendencies. A positive self-concept must take place in your imagination before it will ever be useful in the skirmishes of life. This is cooperating with God's view of us. This is being our own best friend and not a superwoman!

9
How Can I Value Myself?

Choosing to Be Positive

You will feel slightly uneasy making personal affirmations if this has not been your habit pattern. A part of your mind may even be suggesting that this isn't in line with Scripture and you are just becoming arrogant. Any new habit feels awkward until it becomes integrated into your life-style.

It is my belief that we need to align our lives with the positive affirmations and promises of Scripture. Never is God glorified or His people helped as a result of negativity and a critical spirit.

The Holy Spirit seeks positive women who are cooperating with the changes and growth He desires in their lives. He wants women who are in communion with Him through prayer, who through their study of the Word are growing in awareness of their freedoms and possibilities and who are committed to adopting His view of themselves and others. These are women who acknowledge that the cross of Jesus Christ is the ultimate plus sign and who are committed toward growing into positive believers rather than negative ones. Have you ever had the courage to ask a close friend whether she felt you were basically positive or negative in your reactions to life?

I believe there are 10 reasons why we need to choose to be positive.

Positive Christian Women Are Christ-Centered, Not Sin- or Guilt-Centered. Do you often carry around with you a fuzzy feeling of guilt that is impossible to define? Do you find it easier to focus on guilt than on Jesus Christ's love and forgiveness? If you struggle with guilt, there is a marvelous verse I would like to introduce you to: "There is therefore now no condemnation for those who are in Christ Jesus" (Rom. 8:1, *RSV*). Self-inflicted guilt and anger must be dropped if we are going to choose to believe God. Because we have confessed our need for the Saviour and have asked Jesus Christ to be our Lord we are free from divine punishment.

The Holy Spirit does use guilt to convict us. We are pointed, however, to specific areas that need to be changed and can be changed. But God doesn't act as a sledgehammer, as we so often do to ourselves. Through Scripture we are introduced to a fatherly, loving corrector. After our sin is confessed the Lord desires us to change our feelings of guilt for a sense of cleansing and freedom.

Self-punishment and condemnation are *not* to be viewed as God-given feelings. But you aren't the only person who has experienced those unspecific guilt feelings or John wouldn't have written 1 John 3:19-20 *(NASB)*: "We shall know by this that we are of the truth, and shall assure our heart before Him, in whatever our heart condemns us; for God is greater than our hearts, and knows all things."

Through this verse we are assured that even though we may feel condemnation we can positively assure our hearts that God, who has forgiven our sins and cast them into the deepest ocean, is greater than our hearts. If we claim this as truth we will be Christ-centered women.

Positive Christian Women Refuse to Lose Hope. Why? Because where God is, there is always hope. Do you believe that "all things work together for good to those who love God?" If you do the result will be a positive belief, affirming that everything happening in life occurs for your benefit. Learning to accept your realities and working with them is the outward sign of your inward hope. Do you demand that people or circumstances must change in order for you to be happy? There is a heavenly reason for everything in life: may we always learn and grow from our experiences.

This doesn't mean we should say we don't have any problems. Neither does it mean we should expect to be happy in the midst of difficult circumstances. It does mean we can positively affirm that there are no circumstances in our lives which we, as believers in Jesus Christ, cannot use to help our growth. This is our basis for refusing to lose hope.

Positive Christians Accept the Scriptural Truth that Whatever We Sow We Will Also Reap. Proverbs 23:7 *(NKJV)* states "as [a woman] thinks in [her] heart, so is [she]." Positive thoughts lead to positive acts which in turn lead to a positive life-style. What we put into our minds is soon displayed in our lives.

If we dwell on inadequacies we decrease our self-assurance and we destroy a part of ourselves. It may be a small self-criticism to begin with but it often grows into a monstrous, controlling habit. We criticize ourselves first so someone else won't have to. Sometimes we fantasize other people taking pity on us. If this happens we've really got something to be unhappy about. These habits invite even greater negativity into our lives.

There are pay-offs for being negative which we must learn to reject. A person steeped in negativity often lives out the script of a martyr overflowing with self-pity or lives in such a way as if to prove she really is unlovable.

A. Self-rejection is an excuse for not accepting responsibility for my own happiness.

B. I can hide behind a smokescreen of inferiority rather than admitting that I don't know who I am. I only know who I am not.

C. I can avoid the risk of sharing my honest feeings.

D. I can be lazy about maximizing my growth.

E. I can hold on to a bag of self-condemnations in an effort to endear myself to others.

F. I have a perfect justification for continuing to be dependent on others rather than facing life on my own.

G. I have an excellent justification for failure.

H. I have a valuable reason for indulging in self-pity.

I. Satan's off my back. After all, I'm doing his work for him.

Is that the abundant life that Jesus Christ desires for us? Thoreau refers to us as sculptors who have the ability to create the person we want to be. What food are you feeding your thoughts? Whatever you sow you will also reap. Being positive means more than just casting out negative thoughts, although that *is* an important aspect of it. Pause for a moment and answer these questions:

Are you actively looking for the good in yourself, in others and in situations? (See Phil. 4:8.)

Think back on your activities of last week. What magazines and/or books did you read? What TV programs did you watch? What functions did you attend?

What we watch and think has a direct effect on us. Are we suffering from emotional malnutrition because of the diet we have been feeding our eyes, ears and souls? Denis Waitley asks a profound question in his book *Seeds of Greatness:* "If a 60 second commercial, by repeated viewing, can sell us a product, then isn't it possible for a 60 minute soap opera or 'smut-com' by repeated viewing to sell us a life-style?"[1] The Holy Spirit is necessarily limited in His effectiveness in our lives by the choices we make. Whatever we sow we will also reap!

Positive Christian Women Choose the Positive Over the Negative. Our God is a positive God. The Bible is good news. What is your personal focus?

Religion or relationship?
Doubt or faith?
Fear or hope?
Sin or salvation?
Regret or discipline?
Yesterday or today?
Negative or positive?
Crisis or challenge?
Reacting or responding?
Taking chances or making choices?
Impossibilities or possibilities?
Failures or successes?
Blaming or blooming?
Criticizing or creating?
Nightmares or dreams?
Analyzing or affirmation?

When you look in the mirror do you focus on what is wrong or do you notice the things you like? Do you view yourself and others as people who are in the process of becoming all that God wants us to be?

Choose to focus on what the Lord has done in your life rather than on the part not yet finished. Praise and thanksgiving will spring from your lips.

Before reading any further, take the time to chart your spiritual journey to this point in your life. At what age did you commit your life to Christ? How have your relationships affected your faith? Did your educational experience affect your beliefs? Don't just mark the failures. Star the successes that your loving and encouraging Lord has brought into your life.

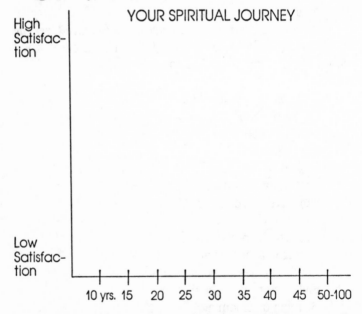

Positive Christian Women Look at the Events in Their Lives As Opportunities to Grow. We often let the events in our lives define for us who we are. If we are divorced we look on our situation as a confirmation that we are a failure; if we are single we assume we are undesirable; if we are happily married we choose to believe we must be acceptable; and if we are unhappily married we feel there is something wrong with us.

The events in our lives only provide opportunities to grow and to learn. They do not determine our identity. God has declared us significant and of value because of Jesus Christ's shed blood, not on the basis of the events in our lives or based on someone else's opinion of them.

It's true, past failures cannot be changed but they can be forgiven. Mistakes as well as successes are learning experiences and stepping-stones in life if we allow them to be. There is no experience in life that we, with the Holy Spirit's assistance, cannot grow from if we choose this perspective.

My family experienced a real tragedy a few years ago. My father is a Presbyterian pastor in Toronto, Canada, and an arsonist broke into his study, taking all the books off Daddy's shelves. He then broke into the file cabinets and removed messages and research from 30 years of study. Next he found all the church hymnals and choir music. After creating a giant pyramid in front of the church altar he set fire to it all. Daddy was wiped out! His comment to me was, "I feel absolutely naked."

After an extraordinarily painful period of shock and denial, my father decided to act on his dream to get his doctorate. He applied to Fuller Theological Seminary in Pasadena, California, and was accepted. With his dream ahead of him and my mother's loving affirmation surrounding him, he began to study as well as maintain his full-time pastoral duties. In June of 1984 at the age of 63, my father received his doctorate. He is living proof that for those who commit themselves to the faithful Lord who gives dreams, beauty does come from ashes. Are you willing for growth to be the result of every event, no matter how hurtful, in your life?

Positive Christian Women Move Out Even When Their Knees are Shaking. Why? Because they have been kneeling on those knees that are shaking. Not only do they know *who* they are they know *whose* they are. Faith is not the absence of fear. Faith involves facing your fears and moving out in God's Power, despite those fears.

Positive Christian women know they accomplish things not because of their fabulous potential but because they are willing to be vessels used by the Lord. They are willing to risk failure and criticism. They are also aware that failure and success are only temporary.

I had to face my personal fear of failure when the Lord first gave me the dream to put my thoughts on self-esteem into book form. Would you believe I fought the dream for six months? I finally asked myself, "What is the worst thing that could happen to you if you failed at writing this book?" When I put the cold hard realities down on paper I decided I could live through possible failure far better than I could live with not carrying out my dream because of the fear of failure. Risking is terrifying, yet the option to shrivel up and die is far worse.

> To laugh is to risk appearing the fool.
> To weep is to risk appearing sentimental.
> To reach out for another is to risk involvement.
> To expose feelings is to risk exposing your true self.
> To place your ideas, your dreams before the crowd is to risk their loss.
> To love is to risk not being loved in return.
> To live is to risk dying.
> To hope is to risk despair.
> To try is to risk failure.

But risks must be taken, because the greatest
    hazard in life is to risk nothing.
The person who risks nothing, does nothing,
    has nothing and is nothing.
He may avoid suffering and sorrow.
But simply cannot learn, feel, change, grow,
    love and live.
Chained by his certitudes, he is a slave.
He has forfeited freedom.
Only a person who risks is free![2]

How we need to understand that not trying is the only failure in life. The only way to keep from making mistakes is to do nothing and that's the biggest mistake of all. We are willing to risk because we are not trying to prove ourselves. Our significance and value has been declared, apart from what we do, by Jesus Christ. That allows us to formulate God's dreams for our world and to act on those dreams, until with the Holy Spirit's assistance, they become reality.

God delights in using human beings with their limitations and inadequacies who are willing to be used. He used Mary, an obscure young girl, to be the mother of His only begotten Son. It becomes evident why Mary was chosen when we read her response to Gabriel: "Behold, I am the handmaid of the Lord; may it be done to me according to your word" (Luke 1:38, *RSV*). She could have argued with the angel and let her negative self-concept be an excuse for not allowing herself to be used. It must have been something to hear an angel say to her, "Hail, favored one! The Lord is with you . . . you have found favor with God." I am so glad that Mary accepted his affirmation and didn't deny it. I'm glad she believed that with God nothing was impossible. I'm glad she was willing to risk. The question to ask yourself now is this: How do your attitudes compare to those of Mary?

Positive Christian Women Don't Stand in Line Waiting for Approval. They Move Beyond by Giving Out Honest Affirmations. We are approved women! The King of Kings and the Lord of Lords has declared it to be so. No longer do we have to stand in line waiting for others to affirm our value. One woman describes it this way in the book *Love* by Dr. Leo Buscaglia:

> Now I know why I am so miserable all the time. It's because I expect to be loved by everyone and that's not possible. I can make myself the most wondrous, the most delectable, the most magical, the most juicy plum in all the world and then there are people out there who are allergic to plums. Then you know what—You make yourself over as a banana because you just met a banana lover. But you'll always be a second-rate banana where you could have been a first-rate plum and just waited for a plum lover to come along.
>
> If you stopped being a plum and concentrated on being a banana then that person thinks that a banana should split and you don't know who you are.[3]

Rather than continually seeking approval the positive Christian woman uses her energy to look for the good in others. Her God-given mission becomes the builder of self-worth in others. She can look for the good in others and tell them about it. This neither threatens her or does she use it as a tool for manipulation because she is free to see the good in herself, too. Likewise, her affirmations are focused not only on what other people do but also on who they are as individuals. They are significant and of great value in God's eyes, and because of that they are significant in her eyes apart from what they accomplish.

Positive Christian Women Make Goals Not Excuses. An interesting exercise for each of us is periodically to keep a running journal of all the excuses we make in any given week for not risking something new or for not achieving some goal. I've discovered through keeping a record of my excuses that my attitude is really what holds me back from being all God and I want me to be. It's yet another illustration of an important truth: What happens *in* us is far more important than what happens *to* us.

One day after reading over all my excuses for not accomplishing things, I grouped my excuses under the topics of negative attitude, procrastination, pettiness, inflexibility, self-pity, worry, laziness, lack of discipline, bad habits and denial. I then went to Scripture to see what God had to say about each one. What an eye-opener! It became crystal clear that God did not want me to limit myself in these ways. Listed below are the excuses I came up with based on my personal experience. Perhaps you have used one or two of these yourself. Are you curious about what Scripture has to say about each of these attitudes?

Attitudes	What God Says
Negative Attitudes	Colossians 3:17 _____
	Philippians 4:8 _____
Excuses	Genesis 3:11-13 _____
	Exodus 4:10-12 _____

Procrastination	Ephesians 5:16 _____
Pettiness	Colossians 3:13 _____
Inflexibility	1 Samuel 15:23 _____
	Proverbs 29:1 _____
Anger	Proverbs 27:4 _____
	Proverbs 27:15 _____
Worry	Philippians 4:6-7 _____
Laziness	Proverbs 24:30-34 _____
Lack of Discipline	Proverbs 25:28 _____
	Galatians 5:22-23 _____
Bad Habits	Hebrews 12:1 _____
Denies Mistakes	Proverbs 28:13 _____

The positive, spirit-filled woman knows it isn't in God's will for her to limit herself. In obedience she stops making excuses and sets goals instead.

Positive Christian Women Assume Personal Responsibility for Their Own Happiness and Self-Esteem. No woman wants to spend the majority of her time being or feeling out of control. Yet many of us have allowed ourselves to slip into this habitual pattern. We are:

- bullied by our emotions
- conned by our circumstances
- whipped by our guilt and "if only's" and

- manipulated by our fantasies about the future.[4]

Often we don't even want to think about the future because we foresee having even less control than we have now. But that is negative imagining.

There are many things positive women acknowledge having control over. We are, for example, responsible for our conversation. A beautiful definition of healthy communication is sharing the truth about ourselves in love. We need to realize that as women we are also responsible, when involved in a relationship, for defining who we are. In addition we need to come to grips with what our needs are, what we think and how we feel. When those things are communicated our conversation is deep and precious.

This type of communication only happens if we take personal responsibility for it. Rather than spending our time trying to control other people by telling them what they should or should not do, we need to learn, through practice, how to communicate the truth about ourselves in love.

There is something we are *not* responsible for, however. We are not responsible for how others act. If your spouse has left you, your children are angry with you, you're divorced, you've been demoted, your friends avoid you or your child is in trouble with the authorities, you cannot conclude that you must be unlovable, a bad parent or a failure who destroys everything she touches. You are only responsible for your actions. You and I are free to choose how we will act but once we have made our choices we are responsible for them.

In Betty Coble's worthwhile seminar and book entitled, *Women Aware and Choosing,* she points out that we are often the happiest when we are doing something we consider to be worthwhile. Our fulfillment often comes as a result of being in charge of our time. A large part of feeling worthwhile is tied into how you feel about the dull, mundane realities of life.

Are you doing something each day you consider worthwhile or are you only doing what everyone else demands that you do? Do you feel as if you are in charge of your time? Certainly there will be days when it seems to get away from you but on the whole, are you in charge? How do you feel about the dull and mundane necessities in your life? Do you ever dream up silly little games to help you get them done faster?

I must confess to allowing myself only 20 minutes to accomplish any given task. If it is necessary I break larger tasks into smaller units. Why? Because then my sense of accomplishment grows as items are checked off my list. Remember, we aren't accomplishing tasks so we can affirm our value. We do these tasks, no matter how mundane, out of a sense of value. Do you tackle the toughest, perhaps least enjoyed assignments, first? May I recommend you do this because you will derive a sense of gratification from having made the effort to do the job. You'll also have additional energy for the remaining tasks.

As Spirit-filled women, we acknowledge that our sense of peace and joy results from our relationship with the Lord Jesus Christ. We also affirm that we, moment-by-moment, choose whether or not to be women who believe God's view of ourselves. Do you remember how you thought you would find happiness as a result of such and such a relationship, or as a result of being married? It is fantasy to believe anyone can make us happy. Rather, we choose to be happy women who share our happiness in each relationship of which we are a part.

If you feel you have no control over your life, look at the Seven C's of Self-Control by Denis Waitley:

1. We Control the Clock. Yes we do. Although it always

runs, we can use it as we choose.

2. We Control Our Concepts. We control our thoughts and creative imaginations.

3. We Control Our Contacts. We can't select all the people we'd like to work with and be with; but we control whom we spend most of our time with and we can meet new people.

4. We Control Our Communication. We are in charge of what we say and how we say it.

5. We Control Our Commitments. We choose which concepts, contacts and communications warrant the most attention and effort.

6. We Control Our Causes. We set our long-range goals in life, which become our causes, and the things we are most identified with by others.

7. We Control Our Concerns. Most people react emotionally to everything they interpret as a threat to their self-worth. Because you and I have a "God-given self-image" (my term) and a deep-down inside feeling of self-worth, regardless of what's going on around us—we respond, rather than react.[5]

I pray each of you will grow in your awareness of your personal responsibility for your own happiness and self-esteem. You make the final decision about whether you will have a positive self-concept or whether you will downgrade yourself with negative, unscriptural and illogical self-talk. You also have the final word to say about your happiness or lack of it. Take the time to ponder the choices you have been making.

Positive Christian Women Seek Out an Affirming Support Group. The Christian woman may choose to affirm the good she sees in others, but she also needs to be affirmed. One woman expressed her need for an affirming support group with these words, "People can't fight my battles nor make my decisions but they can hold me up. They can comfort me, reassure me, cheer me on. So many of our battles have to be fought essentially alone. But it is nice to know that there is a cheering section close by believing in me."[6]

We all need a positive cheering section. My daughter Amy was born at four in the afternoon on the day my support group met. These precious people arrived at the hospital at 6:30 P.M. and prayed over our little girl. Another time someone in our group was going through a season of intense pain. Each member provided food for her and brought little homemade gifts all wrapped up. When the pain was terribly intense she had the joy of opening one of the presents and feeling loved and cared for.

Then there are the goals we share with each other. In our particular group we split up into groups of twos. We exchange our goals, agree to pray over each other's goals daily, phone each other at least once a week and hold one another accountable for personal growth. One can't help but see growth, given that kind of support!

It is such fun to celebrate each other's special days, to pray for each other, to send or receive a surprise postcard of loving affirmation and to be handed a small package to open later as you board a plane for some distant destination. The depth of benefit experienced from receiving and giving such support is tremendously meaningful and can only be measured in the heart.

You've no doubt heard the story of the woman who was about to jump off a high bridge and commit suicide. Another woman came along and the two of them sat down to talk. After an hour, both of them jumped off the bridge. None of us can survive indefinitely if all the voices coming our way are degrading, negative and judgmental. Make it a specific prayer request that the Lord will give you a cheering section and will allow you to be the cheering section for someone else.

Cooperation Is the Key

As a Christian woman you are freed from the necessity to compete. Your assignment is to cooperate with the Holy Spirit and what He wants to do in your life. Christ is present in you in all of His power. This power is waiting to be unleashed in your life if you will cooperate by spending time in God's Word and drinking deeply of God's love, forgiveness and acceptance. You must also spend time praying, praising and choosing to be positive. The question becomes, Am I cooperating with the Holy Spirit's working in my life rather than competing with some perfect standard to prove my worth? In her impatience, the superwoman completely overlooks the truth that growth is a process and processes take time. Think of the years it takes for a seed planted in the earth to blossom into a fruit-producing tree. Christ wants us to go through this process using His strength, not our own. It is so much more satisfying to go through each day aware of God's forgiveness, acceptance, joy, peace, power and love than it is to go through each day competing, failing, and despairing. It is my prayer that on your personal journey towards interdependence you will allow yourself to be transformed from society's superwoman into God's woman. The choice is yours!

Will Others Notice a Difference in Me?

A Call to Serve Others

Throughout the pages of this book the dependent woman, the independent woman and the interdependent woman have been examined. Together we have discovered that we fluctuate in our self-discovery by switching from one mode to another mode, depending on our circumstances. As we seek the Holy Spirit's maturing influences we find ourselves moving more and more towards interdependence and rejecting either dependency or independency as viable options.

The interdependent woman finds her identity first through Jesus Christ's loving sacrifice for her and next through loving God and others. Her self-fulfillment comes as a by-product of loving service. The woman who accepts this as her life's direction will find she is walking a holy walk, not always easy or popular but always growth-producing. She will discover she is walking in her Saviour's footsteps. In Philippians 2:5-8 *(NASB)*, Paul exhorts us to "Have this attitude in yourselves which was also in Christ Jesus, who, although He existed in the form of God, did not regard equality with God a thing to be grasped, but emptied Himself, taking the form of a bondservant, and being made in the likeness of men. And being found in appearance as a man, He humbled Himself by becoming obedient to the point of death, even death on a cross."

Our minds, so often self-centered, can hardly comprehend the fact that the Creator God of our universe would be willing to take on the form of a servant. But that is exactly what He did. He was willing to leave the comfort and honor of heaven to walk through the dust of this earth, to serve the disciples by washing their feet and to rub shoulders with religious and irreligious humanity—who not only didn't believe He was God, but who contemptuously ridiculed Him. He, our God, chose to walk straight to His death on a tree at the hands of mankind which He had created.

Our Lord was also a serving Lord after His resurrection. Recall Christ was on the shore of Lake Galilee, cooking breakfast for seven exhausted disciples who had toiled all night trying to catch fish? A change in His status did not mean a change in His service. Truly Jesus Christ was among us as one who serves (see Luke 22:27). In chapters one through three in the book of Revelation we discover that the risen Lord is the sovereign servant of the Church even today.

As we begin to follow in our Master's footsteps we learn that a commitment to servanthood has to be preceded by a strong sense of identity. Jesus was sure of His identity. He was God! John 10:30 records Christ's words, "I and the Father are one." He didn't have to grasp for deity, He was God. Because He was sure of His identity, He laid aside His position and willingly became human. Only human beings can serve God.

We, as interdependent Christian women, also have a strong sense of identity. We know we are highly significant to God and deeply loved by God. We know we are forgiven and accepted by God because of Jesus Christ's sacrifice and the Holy Spirit's power in us. We don't have to grasp for deity as Satan and Adam and Eve did—we face that tendency in ourselves. We know who we are as God's children and never lose sight of that. Because we are sure of this identity, we can choose to lay aside our rights and willingly become a servant of God and of others.

Apart from the Holy Spirit within us, we give in order to receive, we love in order to be loved and we forgive in order to be forgiven. Servanthood must be the result of the fullness of Christ within us. The story of Mary and Martha serves as a reminder that our service must be because of the fullness of God within us. Otherwise it will be nothing but a duty, an obligation and a real pain.

Service in Worship

We've all been there, haven't we? We've served because we felt it was expected of us, because we wanted to be loved and appreciated, because we wanted to be served in return. It wasn't exactly a joy, was it? We didn't find any fulfillment in it, did we? Fulfillment never comes when our loving and serving is motivated by self. Rather, fulfillment is the result of worshiping our Lord through our service. Peter must have encountered this begrudging attitude because in 1 Peter 4:9 *(NASB)* he admonishes the Christians to "be hospitable to one another without complaint."

If servanthood is indeed our calling, we need to be constantly asking God to fill all of us with all of Him. We need to be filling our minds and spirits with our own Scripture search, with prayer and meditation. We also need times to focus on the wonder of God. Worship releases us from self-centeredness and shows us that freedom comes from dependence on Jesus Christ. Joy is found there. As we spend quality time worshiping the risen Christ and delving deeper into the truth of God's Word we will adopt a servant life-style. We resemble the people we spend most of our time with, don't we?!

Servanthood is the way we identify with our Christ. In Ephesians 5:1-2 *(NASB)* we read this command: "Therefore be imitators of God, as beloved children, and walk in love, just as Christ also loved you, and gave Himself up for us, an offering and a sacrifice to God as a fragrant aroma." In Christ's value system "the greatest among you shall be your servant" (Matt. 23:11, *NASB*). We are called to be imitators of our servant Lord rather than status seekers in the world's system. As we give precedence to God's plan and words in our lives we will discover the truth of finding ourselves through losing ourselves.

Love Knows No Equal Rights

Even though we affirm, as interdependent women, that others are our equals as we are their equals, we acknowledge that as Christ's servants we set aside our equal rights. We willingly, voluntarily, become servants to one another in the Body of Christ because we are identifying with our Lord.

Jesus was equal with God but He didn't cling to His rights. He was willing to risk servanthood so our needs would be met as a result of His sacrifice. He loved us enough to serve us. Can that statement be truly comprehended? Rather than pouting over what He was giving up, Christ chose to concentrate on the people to whom He was giving. Can we do less? So He laid aside His rights and submitted to His Father God's plan. The result came to life when Jesus, the Creator God, knelt in front of mere humans and washed their feet.

One time an admirer asked Leonard Bernstein which instrument was the most difficult to play. Bernstein's answer is classic. "Second fiddle. I can get plenty of first violinists but to find one who plays second violin with as much enthusiasm or second french horn or second flute, now that's a problem. And yet if no one plays second we have no harmony."[1] This illustration hits home because I know how often I find myself building the kingdom of Jan, how often I like the front-row seats, how often I enjoy being center stage and how often I am self-conscious as opposed to God-conscious. The Holy Spirit is actively teaching me lessons about enthusiastically playing second violin. How's the harmony in your home, office and life-style?

Weigh Your Words

Yet another way Christ demonstrated His servanthood was through His verbal availability. We must recognize that our servanthood is demonstrated in the same way. Our words do much to let the people in our lives know if we really are available.

Our words can draw someone near or they can drive them away. They can undergird or undercut, bolster or belittle, demonstrate our respect or disrespect. Words indicate whether we are more concerned with kindness or with always being correct; whether we are more interested in a ministry of reconciliation or in keeping a record of wrongs; whether we are more interested in lecturing or listening; whether we consider it necessary to be responsible for another person's actions or responsible for loving another person; whether our children, husbands or friends are our friends or our foes. Words can encourage or enrage, affirm or attack, betray excitement or exhaustion, demonstrate concern or criticism. They can welcome or wound. Words betray our availability.

When an acquaintance arrives unexpectedly, your husband arrives home or when your children come home from school, what attitudes do your words convey? When you are in the middle of an errand, what do your words and attitude indicate to other people about your availability? Our words betray, as little else does, the value we put on availability. Our attitudes are also highly contagious. Like the measles they reproduce themselves a hundredfold in our lives and they spread into the world around us.

Be a Lover of Life

You've heard the saying that the darker the night is the brighter the stars shine. We are called to be the bright shining stars in our homes, communities and churches and love is the evidence that we are Christ's women, called to be in partnership with our Lord in loving and serving our world.

Even though Christ is the initiator of love while we are the responders, this does not give us license to be passive responders to life. Dependence on our Saviour alone frees us to be the most courageous lovers and servants of our world. In Romans 12:10-13, *(NASB)* we read these words: "Be devoted to one another in brotherly love; give preference to one another in honor; not lagging behind in diligence, fervent in spirit, serving the Lord; rejoicing in hope, persevering in tribulation, devoted to prayer, contributing to the needs of the saints, practicing hospitality."

Service in Hospitality

Servanthood will also be demonstrated through the adventure of hospitality. When I use the word hospitality, do you immediately think of a beautifully set table with a full set of matching china, crystal and sterling silver? I appreciate the beauty of those things but that is not what I am referring to when I use the word "hospitality." I am referring to an *attitude* of being receptive and open to people including my family, friends and even strangers. It involves a willingness to see others from God's point of view as highly significant, deeply loved and valuable in spite of what they do, how they act or what they look like. It involves acknowledging that everything I have, own and am comes from God's hands. It becomes a willingness to share God's blessings with others. Obedience is involved and Paul challenges us to "accept one another, just as Christ also accepted us to the glory of God" (Rom. 15:7, *NASB*).

A very wise person once pointed out that the world is full of either guests or hosts. It seems to me the difference between the two is our willingness to make the world a beautiful place, both physically and emotionally, for other people.

I once experienced some people who felt they were guests in life. It was a Thanksgiving Day, and in accordance with our tradition, we invited people who don't have family close by to our home for dinner. Although each one in attendance was a special person, not one of them was willing to be responsible for initiating conversation, helping to serve the food or clean up afterwards.

When they left I fell into a chair exhausted and asked the Holy Spirit what He was trying to show me. He asked me if I hadn't slipped back into being a guest rather than a host with the people in my life. Without the cross of Jesus

Christ we would all be guests. That cross can transform us into hosts.

How gentle the Holy Spirit has been with this goal-oriented woman, in molding me into a hospitable woman. I certainly was not always willing to be part of the process. When I was a new bride I really wanted to spend all my time with this new husband of mine. He had come from a home that was constantly full of people. I, on the other hand, had come from a home that entertained only a few times a year because of my mother's career plus the responsibility of being a pastor's wife and mother. Well, since Dave was used to a house full of people he thought it was a little quiet with just the two of us. So with my husband as a motivator I started to entertain. What a spread I put on! What a table I set! Trouble was, by the time our friends arrived I was not only exhausted but had usually experienced one or two blow-ups with my hubby. I was not very interested in my guests' emotional state when they arrived. But I certainly wanted their compliments.

Would you believe the next year the Lord placed us in a pastorate? There I was—a minister's wife who viewed people as interruptions. You see, I had a college teaching job for the first time and I wanted to be good at it. At the same time we entertained mostly young people and I found myself doing it a great deal. It couldn't be spectacular because we just couldn't afford to feed myriads of young people that way. I was miserable. I was lonely. I resented the time I didn't have with my husband because of all his church responsibilities. It got so bad I felt I was wasting my time if I spent time talking on the phone.

Eventually we moved on to another position and God in His goodness sent an angel. The woman's name was Irene and she helped the selfish, angry child in me. Dear Irene. Such a gift of hospitality you rarely see. Irene always had time. If you arrived at her home first thing in the morning or late at night she was genuinely glad to see you. If you surprised her, after an initial comment about the state of affairs in her home, she would focus on you as if you were the most important person in her world. She entertained creatively but simply and she wasn't afraid to let you help. People were her main focus.

I was mightily impressed by the fact that Irene was as hospitable to her own family as she was to others. This was not a lady who had nothing to do. In fact, what she accomplished often made my head spin. But people were her focus and she loved us with an accepting, affirming, servant love. As you can guess, Christians and non-Christians alike flocked to her and the Holy Spirit used her to begin a work in me.

Slowly I began to change one thing at a time. The first thing I did was change my menus. Every experience didn't have to be gourmet. Whatever I prepared I attempted to have it completed 20 minutes ahead of the time our guests were to arrive so Dave and I could pray for our friends and the evening. The result of those two decisions was miraculous.

That was the turning point in my life and no longer am I guilty about time spent with others. I now believe that relationships are the most important thing in my world. In fact, I've been told I have the gift of hospitality and I think I do. But I know it's a gift that's been created in me by a loving heavenly Father who cares desperately about His children's relationships.

Perhaps you are naturally a people person. What a wonderful characteristic to have! A people person likes to be around people much of the time and she chooses when she will be alone. A non-people person likes to be alone and chooses when she will be with people. Regardless of our natural inclination, we are all called to serve through the vehicle of hospitality.

One summer we worshiped with a precious group of Christians in Fort Collins, Colorado. On the wall of their multi-purpose auditorium hung a huge banner. The words caught my attention and pulled on my heartstrings: "This is a healing place where inspiration, rest, the love of Christ and the praise of God will lift men's hearts and save their souls."

Dear Lord Jesus, in my attitudes, in my home, through my words, make me a healing place for people to come to. What I serve will be an extension of my creativity but that is really beside the point. Fundamentally important is whether the people in my life have found a healing place of inspiration and rest, where Christ is held up and because of it people are lifted and meet my precious Lord face-to-face. That is hospitality. That is servanthood. Amen.

> For your Holy Spirit, God,
> I'm thankful!
> Without Him, I'm nervous, anxious,
> fearful—too often thinking of me:
>
> What will she think of me?
> How will I impress him?
> Will they think I'm weird?
> What if they don't like my idea?
>
> But oh, how happy I am with your Holy Spirit!
> He focuses my thoughts on You:
> How may I best represent Jesus?
> Will I be careful of His reputation?
> What will be their response
> to His love
> through me?
>
> Release! Support! Affirmation!
> And then comes His serendipity!

In each person He shares with me
He reveals His Son.
He enables me to enjoy their differences!
Because of what He paid for them;
Because of what He's doing within them;
Because He's promised to finish
what He's started in each who chooses Him,
I can love them—
actually enjoy them—
each unique, special creation.

Thanks much, Lord,
for replacing my fear
with your love,
my anxiety
    with enjoyment,
my doubt
    with hope.

Your Spirit is my stronghold!
He is my treasure, my precious friend. [2]

Is It Okay to Be Me?

Examining Mutual Submission

The only woman who is free to submit is the interdependent woman. And when she uses the word "submission" she is referring to the concept of mutual submission
in all her relationships, even her marriage. In her mind
mutual submission is not involuntary subjection, a "trade-
off in domination,"[1] or self-negation. Neither is it a fifty-
fifty relationship, in which she only contributes 50 percent
and the other party does the same, or a relationship which
allows one party to be used as a doormat.

Rather, mutual submission is the result of being filled
with the Holy Spirit. Elaine Stedman defines it in a way I
find personally meaningful:

> Authentic submission is not reluctant nor
> grudging, nor is it the result of imposed author-

ity. It is rather a chosen, deliberate, voluntary, love-initiated response to another's need. It is an act of worship to God, whom we serve in serving others. In no way, then, is authentic submission a violation of our humanity. It is appropriate to the purpose for which we were created, since in serving his creatures we are serving and worshipping our Creator. And it acknowledges the dignity of our humanity because it is service freely rendered from a will surrendered to the loving purpose of God. [2]

Submission is voluntary—a personal choice—and is only possible for those women and men who have a strong understanding of who they are. Mutual submission is only possible between two people who are aware of their equality before God and each other. The need for mutual submission is clear, for it is impossible to share our faith in Jesus Christ by word and by example with someone we are treating as a doormat or with someone we have placed on a pedestal.

Mutual submission results from our awareness that in serving others, we are really serving and worshiping our God. It is possible only when we believe the command "Be ye . . . perfect, [whole, complete, fulfilled] even as your Father which is in heaven is perfect [whole, fulfilled, complete]" (Matt. 5:48, *KJV*) was given to both men and women. Therefore both members in the relationship will do their best to develop and affirm each other's gifts, talents, wholeness and completeness. They are also willing to improve their communication skills—the ultimate tool of mutual submission.

It is not my purpose in this book to delve into the biblical and historical arguments about submission. If you desire a thorough study from a biblical perspective, may I recommend the book, *Heirs Together* by Patricia Gundry. My purpose is to show how dependent and independent women misunderstand and misuse God's plan of submission. And, although this chapter carefully analyzes submission in the marital relationship, the information can be applied to our friendships and family relationships.

The Dependent Woman

The dependent woman has lost her sense of wholeness. She specializes in addictive relationships as a result. Her only sense of identity, apart from her relationships, is negative and inferior. Therefore she defines herself in relation to others, depending on *them* to determine her sense of self. She is the little girl always trying to earn someone's approval and pushes for uniformity in her relationships because that makes her feel secure.

The dependent woman is all too happy to turn over the controls of her life to a man—or so it seems. Since throughout her dating years she has repressed her true self, it appears she will submit to the man in a marital relationship, becoming what he wants her to be and repressing her true self.

In his book *How to Become Super-Spiritual or Kill Yourself Trying* John Sterner describes a woman who has opted for dependency:

> Suzy Submissive is totally dedicated to the care and feeding of her husband's ego. Each day of Suzy's life is filled with plans: She plans food that Fred will enjoy, sex that will excite him, and conversation that will be stimulating to him. She plans a fulfilling life for Fred.
>
> Suzy read somewhere that wives are supposed

to submit to their husbands (Eph. 6) and she has been doing it ever since. The trouble is, Suzy is rapidly losing her personality, her friends and her cool. Her conversation is loaded with "Fred says" and "Fred thinks." Suzy has stopped thinking. She has also stopped going to church because Fred thought she was becoming too religious. She watches only the T.V. programs Fred likes and she has stopped seeing any friends Fred does not care for. She has for all practical purposes, stopped living.[3]

Does submission mean destroying our individuality and never rocking the boat? The dependent woman believes that is exactly what it means. After all, this is how she lives.

May I introduce you to three dependent women who are submissive.

June met and married her husband while she was in her late teens. She put him through school by working in a department store—a job she continued to hold until he became fairly established in a new business. She then stopped working altogether due to an insistent and very persuasive Bible teacher who was certain the woman's place was in the home. Eventually two little children came along and now at the age of 45 June doesn't know who she is or what she wants out of life. All she knows is this: she wants more than she's got. Absolutely nothing makes her content, even though she keeps quite a frantic schedule teaching home Bible studies.

June's reactions to her life are drastic and debilitating. The loneliness caused by her ever-absent husband is wearing on June and she feels unappreciated and unloved most of the time. Her husband has not lived up to her expectations and she is deeply depressed. In fact, she is spending more and more time in bed due to one "illness" or another. Her house is in a shambles and she is developing an ulcer from all the inner turmoil and anger she feels. On top of all this she has a gnawing fear in her heart that her husband is going to leave her. This thought almost suffocates her so she clings tighter and tighter to her man—even though the life she clings to makes her miserable.

Monica is single and hates every second of it. All of her life, her mother has told her she is nothing without a man and Monica has swallowed her mother's philosophy hook, line and sinker. Monica believes in her heart of hearts that men are superior so she doesn't live her own life. Instead she gives her life to any available man, always hoping this will be the one to complete her. Since she doesn't enjoy her own company nor trust her own judgments or intellect, she latches onto someone who will provide the goals, rules and orders for her life. She spends her life being someone else's person, with no self-identity. Needless to say, Monica is miserable. Because she considers herself to be only half a person she is continually attracted to men who are only half-men. Her latest romance was with a traveling salesman whom she later learned was married.

Carol is a beautiful woman who also happens to be a talented musician. Carol was headed toward a masters degree in music when she first met her future husband, Dave. He was threatened by her gifts and she responded by erasing *her* academic goals and nurturing *his* dream—to become a pastor.

The concept of oneness has always appealed to Carol. She believed she not only took her husband's name but also his identity. In Carol's case this means being a pastor's wife!

If Carol is really honest there is a part of her that has never really wanted to grow up. When she first met Dave she was looking for a man who would care for her. She still wants this today. In her own words, "I need a man to lean on, to tell me I'm okay."

Rather than accepting God's approval as well as searching internally for her own approval, she needs her husband's affirmation to prove her self-worth. Being a busy, preoccupied and often threatened pastor, Dave has little affirmation to give. Nevertheless Carol waits like a small child for his nod of approval.

Carol is increasingly afraid to stand up for what she believes because her husband might be threatened and she might become unacceptable in his eyes. Out of this fear she refuses to communicate the truth in love about herself. She is so terrified of rejection she can't say no to anything her husband wants and is at his beck and call 24 hours a day. She consoles herself by saying, "It could be worse. I could be single."

The Payoffs

June, Monica and Carol are dependent in their relationships with the men in their life. But there are payoffs from dependency and don't let anyone tell you there are not. First, the dependent woman feels cared for and safe. She doesn't have to grow up. Since she is familiar with what it means to be taken care of by parents she is quite content to let a man take care of her, too.

Second, it is possible for her to feel more spiritual when she uses self-blame and self-punishment. This is the height of arrogance because Jesus Christ has already bled and died as a sacrifice for our sin. The dependent woman somehow believes she can add to Christ's sacrifice.

Staying dependent also involves laziness and this is the third payoff for dependent women and Satan alike. He will either persuade you you're fine as you are or you're so very rotten you can't possibly change. It is then easier and safer for the dependent woman to stay the same. The hard work of setting goals to change attitudes, thoughts, feelings and actions can be avoided. This woman is certainly no threat to Satan, is she!

As long as these women are able to blame others, they won't have to change. They will also get a great deal of sympathy from people which promotes continual denying, repressing and suppressing of the issues. She chooses to live in a personal fantasyland, never *really* desiring to change.

Women who believe that dependency and submission are one and the same have often learned this style of submission at their church. Therefore they believe dependency to be the Lord's pattern for their life.

The Dependent Woman's Lethal Weapons of Control

But here is a trap and how easy it is to fall into it. A woman can *pretend* submission. How often have you heard a woman say something like, "He may be the head of this home but I'm the neck that moves the head"? These women affirm their husbands by saying, "Whatever he says is right, after all he is the leader." But how they dishonor their husbands and themselves through their actions.

The dependent woman's lethal weapons of control are manipulation and retaliation. Notice the small step separating *being controlled* from *being controlling.* These women are the pussycat manipulators who resent their own lack of control so much they get back at their man—any way they can.

One manipulative method involves suffocating their men with kindness by babying them. By refusing to be honest about any issue or conflict, the dependent woman protects her man from self-understanding. She picks out everything from his suits to his deodorant and how she delights in making excuses for him. The children, for example, are not to bother their father with their problems because he is exhausted and works much too hard. She babies him because she is terrified of change. This can be avoided if he remains the same.

She can be dishonest with her words and actions. While claiming to be submissive and a follower she can destroy her husband's financial base by wasting their money with unwise purchases. She can talk disparagingly to him by reminding him of every irresponsibility—every way he hasn't shaped up to fit her expectations. She can also choose to be disrespectful and divisive—like the pastor's wife I knew as a child, who refused to go anywhere her husband was preaching. She can subtly shame him, use sex to manipulate him, silence to frustrate him, use guilt trips to condemn him, self-pity and nagging to overwhelm him and a poor state of health to blackmail him. She often waits until her man gives an opinion before subtly opposing him.

These women are dependent on their men but their need for men is unhealthy. They seek personal security in their man but indulge, flatter and attempt to buy them any way they can. In other words, they become masters of manipulation. It almost happens in self-defense, for no woman or man can experience emotional health when their sense of self is defined by someone else.

The Independent Woman

This is the woman who reacts with horror to the concept of submission. Antagonized as she is about the misuse of submission, she "throws out the baby with the bathwater" and isolates herself.

Although the dependent woman receives some payoffs from manipulating her partner within a submissive relationship, the independent woman experiences a temporary payoff by rejecting submission altogether. She feels in touch with herself and believes she is in control of her life by accepting relationships on her own terms and doing things her way. She ignores 1 Corinthians 11:11, *NASB* which says, "However, in the Lord, neither is woman independent of man, nor is man independent of woman."

A middle-aged woman recently shared with me how she had decided to nurture her career rather than intimate relationships. She sold out to the business establishment and rose quickly up the corporate ladder—at the expense of healthy intimacy, however. Two relationships had been important to her at one time but not so precious that she would make any concessions for them after her decision to make business her life. Eventually her personal relationships faded away. There she sat, beautifully groomed and financially comfortable but absolutely alone. She certainly had offers but only, it seemed to her, from people who wanted to use her for their pleasure or to further their career. She was absolutely miserable. There are no payoffs ultimately for total independence!

The Interdependent Woman

Friendship with the interdependent woman may not always be as easy as a relationship with the "yes, whatever you want" or dependent type of woman. Because both people in a relationship happen to be Christians does not insure that their values will always be similar. There may also be wide differences between husbands and wives. But it is in the face of conflict, which is inevitable when two thinking people are involved in a relationship, that the principle of mutual submission shines. How fascinating it is to find out what each other is like.

James Fairfield has created a diagram illustrating five fairly normal styles of relating.[4]

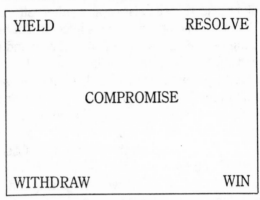

When one person in the relationship constantly WINS and the other one YIELDS it shows a low concern for the relationship and each other. The person who consistently yields is repressing his or her thoughts, feelings and opinions. This is unbiblical and unhealthy.

If one person or both people WITHDRAW from the conflict, that also shows a low regard for the relationship. They are just not willing to stick in there and communicate. They may also be terribly afraid.

The COMPROMISE position, or what I call the "horse-trading" position ("If you do this, I will do this . . . ") shows a slightly higher regard for the relationship—but it is not the ideal.

It is the RESOLVE position we are headed for. If an issue is to be resolved, both people must be willing to hear what the other person feels and thinks along with the reason he or she holds that opinion. Both individuals then examine the positives and negatives of each position and finally settle on a resolve which both find satisfying. This is a verbal picture of mutual submission.

I am nothing but you are a person of worth and dignity. (dependent) (unhealthy submission)		I am a person of worth and dignity and you are a person of worth and dignity. (mutual submission) (interdependent)

YIELD   RESOLVE

COMPROMISE

WITHDRAW   WIN

I am nothing and you are nothing. (No regard for a relationship, self or other).		I am a person of worth and dignity but you are expendable. (interdependent) (authoritarian)

The ultimate goal is to work each conflict through to the resolve position. It often takes time to get there. Waiting until each side can get more facts and a more educated solution might be the best move. If that seems to be impossible the couple must compromise, change direction or work it through together until they come to a mutually agreeable solution. If one person has greater expertise in one area, by all means call on that knowledge and agree together to use it. Free that person up to make decisions in their area of expertise.

As Christian women we need to be willing to take the first step toward reconciliation. Never is our motivation for reconciliation to establish a position of superiority or to acknowledge inferiority. We choose reconciliation as our goal out of obedience to our Lord and because we value ourselves, the other person and the relationship.

Benefits and Blessings

This type of relationship, as I have stressed before, will not always be easy but the benefits will be overwhelming. I've included 17—do you have any to add to the list?

1. *It frees us up to be ourselves.* If we are married, our husbands fell in love with a spunky, interesting woman. Mutual submission gives us the freedom to be that woman for a lifetime. "It allows both husband and wife to contribute to the union from the richness of all that they are. It allows both mates to contribute all their abilities and attributes."[5]

2. *We become real in each situation.* It forces us to get in touch with ourselves. Our feelings, thoughts, dreams and questions suddenly take on a new importance.

3. *We become much better listeners.* We genuinely care about other people's feelings, thoughts, dreams and questions. This makes us a more effective communicator.

4. *We acknowledge equal rights in a relationship.* David Augsburger and John Faul comprehensively define what this means:

I am free to choose my words and acts;
Therefore free to change and grow.

I am free to be spontaneous;
Therefore free to make mistakes.

I am free to trust my hunches;
Therefore free to be illogical.

I am free to be flexible;
Therefore free to change my mind.

I am free to live by my own supports;

Therefore free to refuse help and kindness.

I am free to take the consequences for my
acts;
Therefore free to offer no justification for
my choices.

I am free to love and care for others;
Therefore free to tell you without permission.

I am free to want relationships;
Therefore free to reach out for contact.[6]

5. *We become affirmers to others just as our Lord is to us.* We learn to help other people believe that their dreams can become reality. Each person is helped to find, cherish and develop all that they are. Luke 6:31 (*TLB*) puts it this way, "Treat others as you would want them to treat you."

6. *Mutual growth is a result.* As long as one person is not free to grow the other partner won't achieve his full potential either. Both partners are helped to deepen, grow and change.

"When husbands and wives live the way Jesus did, they do not play out roles in which one or the other hides away a part of himself or herself in order not to be upset or displease the other. They trust God will be in their every move and then they move—even if it rocks the boat."[7]

7. *We value each other equally as persons.* We acknowledge we are both equally important to God, to each other and to the relationship. We mirror that belief through our actions.

8. *Unity rather than conformity becomes an important value to each person.* Harmony is considered far healthier than being a revised standard version of someone else.

9. *Each partner owns his own emotions, expressions, experiences, actions and happiness or lack of it.* As a result he is not emotionally controlled by the other person or absorbed with the other person.

10. *Both partners treat each other with equal respect for they are "heirs together" of God's grace.* Both people are valuable, therefore they will refuse to take advantage of each other nor will they be possessive of each other. Feelings of intimacy and trust are heightened.

11. *We become equal in opportunity.* Both partners are free to be involved in ministries. Christ's world is in front of both of us and He cheers us on while we cheer each other on.

12. *Together we assume personal responsibility for the style of our marriage.* There is no longer a need to live by someone else's formula.

13. *Our children become God's children,* entrusted into our keeping for only a short time. One person is not solely responsible

for the raising of them. Neither is one partner cheated of the joy of really knowing his
children as people.

14. *We will gain increased feelings of self-confi-
dence* as a result of accepting our God-
given identity and maturing as the Holy
Spirit directs. We will no longer be domi-
nated by others.

15. *We will be increasingly dependent on the
Lord Jesus Christ* because we refuse to be
dependent on someone else for our spiritual growth and personal development.

16. *The manipulation comes to a swift halt.*
Instead, I give you the very best I have to
give. I lift you up because we are equals. I
serve you with joy because I love. We are
free. Ponder these words by Nancy R.
Smith:

"For every woman who is tired of acting
weak
    when she knows she is strong,
there is a man who is tired of appearing
strong
    when he feels vulnerable;

"For every woman who is tired of acting
dumb,
there is a man who is burdened with the
constant
    expectation of 'knowing everything;'

"For every woman who is tired of being
called
    an 'emotional female,'

there is a man who is denied the right to weep
and to be gentle;

"For every woman who is called unfemi-nine
when she competes,
there is a man for whom competition is
the only way to prove his masculinity;

"For every woman who is tired of being a sex object,
there is a man who must worry about his potency;

"For every woman who feels 'tied down' by her
children,
There is a man who is denied the full plea-sure of
shared parenthood;

"For every woman who is denied mean-ingful employment
or equal pay,
there is a man who must bear full financial
responsibility for another human being;

"For every woman who was not taught the intricacies
of an automobile,
there is a man who was not taught the sat-isfaction
of cooking;

"For every woman who takes a step toward her own
liberation,[8]

there is a man who finds the way to freedom has
    been made a little easier."[9]

17. *Each partner takes responsibility for the
home.* No longer is it only the wife's
responsibility to keep house, hold an outside job, raise the children and be a respon-
sive mate. Therefore, she is freed from the
necessity to be a superwoman. Rather,
each partner takes personal responsibility
for some of the mundane chores that need
to be done in any home.

Dave and I find that Sunday evening, after our children
have been put to bed, is a good time for us to make mutual
submission a reality in our marriage. First, we share our
individual calendars for the next week. We share our feelings about the week and the pressures that lie ahead of us.
Next, we examine each other's commitments and review
our list of the mundane chores that need to be accomplished around our home. I know you face some of the
same things each week in your home: laundry that needs
to be done, floors that need to be vacuumed and scrubbed
and furniture that must be dusted—along with the grass
and flowers that never take into account how busy you
are! We divide up these necessities, making certain that
there are a few items on our individual lists we enjoy
doing. If your children are old enough, I suggest you
include them during part of your planning time. It is their
home, too.

We also find this a helpful time to check the goals we
have created for ourselves, our *marital* relationship, our
spiritual growth and our children's development. This is
the time to check up on how we feel we did during the last

week. It is necessary to examine whether our goals are realistic and if they aren't, to re-evaluate them. Then we spend a precious time in prayer, committing each other and our week to the Lord and thanking the Lord for the gift of each other.

Lest you think that we have always done this, let me hasten to point out that this tradition in our marriage came out of total failure and frustration. At first this meeting time provided us with a way of coping with an unhealthy situation. It was in the process we discovered, with the Lord's leading, that we had stumbled onto something valuable. Feel free to use our idea or modify it to fit your personal situation.

Before we progress any further let's examine the habit patterns you have established in your relationship.

My Style of Relating

Dependent Life-style
What percentage of the time do you:

	95%	75%	50%	25%	5%
1. Deny yourself the joy of knowing yourself?					
2. Deny others the joy of knowing you and growing with you?					
3. Own your feelings, thoughts and dreams?					

	95%	75%	50%	25%	5%
4. Hesitate to express opinions leading to conflict?					
5. Find that your need to be liked is greater than your need to be honest?					
6. Allow others to manipulate you?					
7. Have a difficult time saying no?					
8. Feel other people are more important than you are?					
9. Feel powerless to change yourself or situations?					
10. Find yourself comparing yourself with others and always coming out on the low end of the totem pole?					
11. Talk about yourself in a self-negating way?					

12. Feel used, taken advantage of, resentful and retaliatory?					
13. Feel you would be helpless if something hap-pened to your mate?					
14. Feel you are liv-ing someone else's life for them?					
15. Feel you are the caretaker of your husband's emo-tional needs?					
16. Value conformity over unity?					
17. Feel inhibited by your relation-ships?					
18. Feel bound by your labels, not knowing who you are apart from what you do?					
19. Feel your partner (or friend) is an authoritarian tyrant?					

	95%	75%	50%	25%	5%
20. Feel you are unusually harsh on yourself?					

Independent Life-style

	95%	75%	50%	25%	5%
1. Find yourself getting your own needs met at any cost?					
2. Find yourself seeking to manipulate and control others?					
3. Feel superior to other people?					
4. Feel judgmental of others? Feel they are finished products?					
5. Own your feelings, thoughts and dreams?					
6. Seek after conflict?					
7. Blame other people or situations for your state of affairs?					

	95%	75%	50%	25%	5%
8. Feel you are more important than other people?					
9. Tell people off?					
10. Expect the worst from others?					
11. Find yourself trying to control others?					
12. Feel hostile?					
13. Communicate the truth in hostility by using "you" statements? (Example: You never . . .)					

Interdependent
Life-style

1. Feel like you are a person who counts?					
2. Own your own feelings, thoughts and dreams?					

	95%	75%	50%	25%	5%
3. Accept yourself as in process?					
4. Accept others as in process?					
5. Feel equal to other people?					
6. Refuse to be intimidating?					
7. Refuse to be intimidated?					
8. Feel honest?					
9. Believe your relationships are based on love rather than guilt, manipulation or fear?					
10. Define your own needs?					
11. Communicate the truth in love by using "I" statements?					
12. Feel your relationships help you to understand yourself?					

	95%	75%	50%	25%	5%
13. Take responsibility for yourself and not someone else?					
14. Confront when necessary?					
15. Feel you are a significant person apart from the labels you wear or what you can accomplish?					
16. Define your own roles?					
17. Respect yourself and others?					
18. Choose to be affirming of yourself and others?					
19. Choose to serve out of love?					
20. Choose to be a participant in mutual submission?					
21. Risk new ideas and growth?					
22. Feel free to be vulnerable?					

	95%	75%	50%	25%	5%
23. Feel spontaneous and real?					
24. Confront in love when appropriate?					
25. Feel like an excellent listener?					
26. Refuse to be a revised standard version of anyone else?					
27. Feel you have equal opportunity to do what you believe the Lord wants you to do?					
28. Feel parenthood is a shared responsibility?					
29. Experience increased feelings of self-confidence?					
30. Experience an increased dependency on the Lord?					

Promoting Change Negatively

I hope you find yourself moving away from the dependent and independent life-style and moving toward the interdependent one. It is in this style of relating that you will discover the beauty of mutual submission. But what if you are locked in a relationship resembling anything but mutual submission? Do you want to bring about change?

First of all, let me point out there are some terribly unhealthy ways to communicate your desire for a change in your relationship. In fact, using these methods shows we are still operating from the dependent or independent mode.

We will never be able to *nag* our mates into changing and my dictionary gives the reason why. Nagging is defined as "persistent petty faultfinding, scolding or urging." Let's take a moment to examine just how clever we have become at the game of nagging. First, by betraying our basic lack of trust in him, we often nag our husbands for not doing something he hasn't had a fair chance to accomplish. A second method is to ask a question we *know* the answer but really don't *like* the answer: "Why aren't you like so and so?" "Why won't you change jobs?" Third, we nag our partner over something that has absolutely nothing to do with what is really upsetting us. Let's establish right now that nagging does not work. A man will never be drawn toward mutual submission if the tool used is nagging.

Nor will he be drawn toward submission if we use *false flattery* to move him in that direction. He may put up with it for a short time because it's certainly better than nagging but he knows you are not speaking the truth to him. This leads to feelings of mistrust—and mutual submission can never be built on that foundation.

The last tool we often delight in using, when the other

two methods have failed, is *outright judgment.* Rather than using the desirable "I" statements like, "I feel . . . ," "I think . . . ," "I need . . . ," "I would enjoy . . . ," we switch into a judgmental attack position. Suddenly everything we say has a dagger in it. Our words and attitudes are accusatory—"You never . . . ," "You always . . . ," "You're such a . . . "—and let him know that we think he's inferior, dull and generally stupid. We usually use this when we are afraid he will never change. Our goal of mutual submission seems blocked and we're furious.

Promoting Change Positively

Does instant success happen very often in your life? It certainly doesn't in mine. Give your partner *time and room* to grow. Allow him his thoughts, feelings, questions and opinions. After all, he was created in the image of God, too. Pray that the Lord will change him. Then acknowledge *your* willingness to grow and change, too.

Use this transition time to really *get in touch with yourself.* Own your feelings, thoughts and beliefs and share these lovingly with your partner. Express why you feel the way you do. If he is open to doing some reading with you, by all means read some books and articles together taking the time to listen to his perspective on the issue. Who knows? You might even grow as a result!

Remind him, in the midst of these times, that you are vitally *concerned with his needs as a man* and as a husband. Even in the midst of conflict, remember to treat him as the highly significant and valuable human being he is. Why? Because that is the way Jesus Christ looks at you.

Sometimes our husbands refuse to be of assistance around the house, for example, because they're unwilling to admit they don't know how to be of help. Perhaps as a child or even as an adult when he did help, someone always criticized the way he assisted. Maybe your husband does help but has such a bad attitude you almost wish that he wasn't part of the work team! Women, who says that either of you has to enjoy everything that needs to be done? He is responsible for his own happiness or unhappiness. You are not. If he chooses to be miserable let him be. Affirm him for his assistance anyway.

Press On Toward the Mark

This will not be an easy stage for you. Growth rarely is easy. Change is not comfortable. The familiar pattern, even if totally destructive and confining, always feels more secure and comfortable. Somehow it feels right even when it is wrong.

Being married is a mutual growing experience. The biblical principle, which frees both partners in the marriage to be all that they can be, is the concept of mutual submission. Rather than suppressing each other, we are free to serve and help each other in love with the Holy Spirit's presence active in our lives. When our marriages begin to move in that direction the road may not always be smooth, but the journey becomes an extremely fulfilling one for both partners.

> I love you
> Not only for what you are,
> But for what I am
> When I am with you.
>
> I love you
> Not only for what
> You have made of yourself,
> But for what
> You are making of me.

I love you because you
Are helping me to make
Of the lumber of my life
Not a tavern,
But a temple;
Out of the works
Of my everyday
Not a reproach,
But a song.

I love you
For the part of me
That you bring out;
I love you
For putting your hand
Into my heaped-up heart
And passing over
All the foolish, weak things
That you can't help
Dimly seeing there,
And for drawing out
All the beautiful belongings
That no one else had looked
Quite far enough to find. [10]

12
We're Free to Be Interdependent Women

Looking Up, Looking In, Moving Out

They came to Bethsaida, and some people brought a blind man and begged Jesus to touch him. He took the blind man by the hand and led him outside the village. When he had spit on the man's eyes and put his hands on him, Jesus asked, "Do you see anything?"

He looked up and said, "I see people; they look like trees walking around."

Once more Jesus put his hands on the man's eyes. Then his eyes were opened, his sight was restored, and he saw everything clearly (Mark 8:22-25, *NIV*).

Looking Up

Although this passage refers to a blind man in Jesus' day I, too, have been that blind man. Years ago my precious family and friends brought a questioning, struggling, intellectualizing young woman to Jesus Christ so she could be touched by His forgiving love and complete acceptance.

Knowing Christ Intimately

Jesus took me away from the familiar and into a land where I was to walk by faith, not by sight. He took me out of myself and confronted me with His reality. He quieted my excessive chatter and replaced it with wonder. He showed me that the search for truth was as important as either the questions or the answers. Christ introduced me to a process of searching for truth rather than giving me a packaged product. He assured me, through the words of the Apostle Paul, that "He who began a good work in you will bring it to completion at the day of Jesus Christ" (Phil. 1:6, *RSV*).

Over the last 15 years of knowing Jesus intimately, I have come to recognize different levels of seeing. When Christ first touched me I became aware of reality as I had never experienced it before. I felt liberated, but I saw only partial truth. The blind man puts it so profoundly, "I see people, they look like trees walking around."

Then as time progressed and I searched the Scriptures, I acknowledged my personal need for a constant filling by the Holy Spirit. I grew as a result of teaching, friendships and circumstances and my vision began to clear. My sight has not been totally restored, nor my perspective made crystal clear. No doubt the place where all the scales will fall from my eyes will be in heaven. But I am at a point in my life where my sight has undergone a transformation. Meeting Christ has made a dramatic difference in my life-style as I pray it will in yours. My view of God, myself and others has changed as a result of knowing Jesus intimately.

When I was first brought to this beautiful Christ I committed what I knew of myself to what I knew of Him. I was still the center of my attention, however. Christ was invited into my life and He accepted my invitation as He will yours: Here I am! I stand at the door and knock. If anyone hears my voice and opens the door, I will go in and eat with him and he with me" (Rev. 3:20, *NIV*). But I didn't know my new Friend enough to trust Him completely. I had heard much of His love but I had also heard much of His holiness and anger. I knew little of His acceptance. So I added Christ to my already hectic schedule. I thought, *I not only need the time to do all the other things that are a part of my life-style, I am also supposed to have time to read this new Friend's love letter, talk to Him and meet with His Body here on earth. How can I ever fit it all in?*

Needless to say I couldn't. But the Holy Spirit does a work in us, sometimes in spite of us. Here is a picture the transformation He brought into my view of priorities:

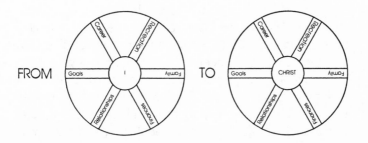

As I experienced the trustworthiness of Christ, the forgiveness of my Saviour and the accepting grace of my Redeemer, I, like Martha, was gently rebuked for having my priorities reversed. As I learned that God views me as deeply fallen but also a highly significant and greatly loved woman, I came to see that God always gives us the very best that He has. Very quickly transformations began in my life.

I began to understand the importance of making Christ central so the other things in my life, as important as they were, didn't become a distraction. Faith and worship and love of God became the hub, as it were, with the other things flowing from it. Everything in my life now has become an opportunity for communion with my Saviour, for He has truly become the unifying, centralizing and cohesive force in my life. My eyes were touched by Christ so my focus would switch away from religious activities and onto a life-style of worship.

When Christ touched my eyes, as He did the blind man's, not only did my view of God and His place in my life change, but so did my view of myself. Because I had swallowed the world's lie that I had no real value unless I earned it, I had let the events of my life define who I was. See diagram on the following page to see how I picture it.

As the Holy Spirit gently but firmly shows me that I am a cherished child of the Living God, I have come to realize what an indestructible support system I have. The God who knows me at the deepest, most intimate levels, even better than I know myself, loves me the most. Because of this awesome knowledge I have come to view the events in my life as opportunities to grow and learn, not as measuring sticks to determine my identity. My identity was settled at the cross.

But not only are my views of God and myself revolutionized as Christ becomes dearer to me, so are my views

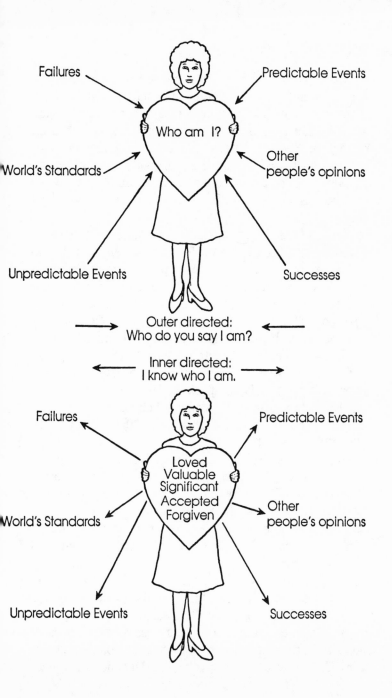

Failures

Predictable Events

Who am I?

World's Standards

Other
people's opinions

Unpredictable Events

Successes

Outer directed:
Who do you say I am?

Inner directed:
I know who I am.

Failures

Predictable Events

Loved
Valuable
Significant
Accepted
Forgiven

World's Standards

Other
people's opinions

Unpredictable Events

Successes

of others. Because I have truly grasped God's forgiveness and acceptance, I can let go of my confessed guilt. Now, with my new support system, I don't have to build my life around other people, be it my husband, friends, children or myself. Because I have been declared equal and adequate, I don't need to prove I am as good as any other man or woman. I don't need to make myself an object of worship because I worship the Christ, the son of the living God.

Just as I am a cherished child of God, so is every other person. I respect God's priceless investment in each and every person. I see the futility of pretending to be better than I am, for mutually we are all God's children. Possessiveness, uniformity, pretense and manipulation are to have no part in my life-style. Rather than seeing through each other, each of us is called to see each other through.

Using people to promote my image, my dreams and my plans is always manipulative. I am to use things, not people. When I truly comprehend that we are all part of one Body, I realize that any damage I choose to do to other Christians not only hurts them, it also hurts Christ and is ultimately self-destructive.

As we *look up,* we experience God's touch on our lives. Just as the blind man's vision and perspective changed, so will ours. With Paul, who had been in the ministry 25 years, we will breathe out our deepest desire: "that I may know him and the power of his resurrection" (Phil. 3:10, *RSV*). The yearning of our hearts is satisfied by Christ alone.

Finally, as I come to know Christ more intimately I am able to see that I am not a victim of the events in my life but a child of God, placed on this earth to love the people in my life. In the process of loving I can affirm their value apart from their performance. I can affirm our equality in Christ. I can warn those involved in dependent and independent relationships and encourage, with the Holy Spirit's filling, interdependent relationships—all as a result of knowing Him.

Looking In

We who are privileged to be Christian women have an excellent God. We who are representatives of the Lord Jesus Christ are involved in a purpose bigger than ourselves. We are His vehicle to provide hope to our hurting world.

Our purpose is vast. We are ordinary women but when we dare to join forces with an extraordinary God, we find ourselves pursuing excellence, shooting for the stars and daring to be the best we can possibly be. In Ecclesiastes 9:10 *(NASB)* we read these words: "Whatever your hand finds to do. . . do it with all your might." A pastor put it this way, "Pray as if it all depends on God and work as if it all depends on you."

During the writing of this chapter the Twenty-third Olympiad was being held in Los Angeles. I was thrilled by the dedication, sometimes in spite of unbelievable odds, the young athletes exercised. The results were evident in their strong, courageous, healthy bodies. We sometimes forget that we, too, are in a race—a race for a goal far more valuable than gold. Are we living our lives as if the Olympic games were an every day reality in our lives?

Are we aware that without Christ we can do nothing (John 15:5) but with Christ we can do all things? Each one of us needs an impossible dream to keep us alive—a dream that will take Christ to make it happen.

Do you have such a dream? Have you dared to get to know yourself well enough that you can define what are the desires of your heart? Or have you denied your personal needs for so long that panic has begun to strike when you read this section?

Remember that God "is able to do exceeding abundantly above all that we ask or think . . . " (Eph. 3:20, *KJV*) if we let Him. So let's join forces with our miracle working God in the pursuit of excellence.

Even when we commit ourselves to a dream it is possible to be sidetracked from our original intention. In order to avoid having this happen, there are 10 things we need to do on a continual basis in our lives.

1. Scrutinize Your Life-style, Gifts and Abilities

God wants you to be your own unique, unrepeatable person, not just a carbon copy of someone else. Since He, as it were, broke the mold when He made you, there is a particular position in His kingdom you can fill.

Take stock of who you are. Pause and reminisce for a short time. What experiences have you had in your lifetime? Take the time to list these no matter how insignificant they seem.

If you had unlimited resources, what types of things would you most enjoy doing? List these interests. What abilities do you have? This is not the time for negative thinking or downgrading yourself. Make a list. If you are having difficulty ask people who love you to help you. What spiritual gifts has the Lord created in you? Ask women whose wisdom you treasure to help you identify your gifts.

What kind of books do you enjoy reading? What new classes might you be interested in taking? What hobbies do you enjoy? What would you like people to say about you if they were summing up your life? What are the opportunities you have at your fingertips? What volunteer work have you done? Make a list.

If, as you are doing this, you are feeling a mounting

pressure to be a superwoman, stop! Each of our lives have seasons, and with the advent of each new season we are able to accomplish different goals. Never do we accomplish all of them at one time, so relax. Remove any of the "shoulds" you are putting on yourself and continue to brainstorm.

Perhaps you have young children and you have chosen to stay at home while they are young. This season of your life may be as short as five years or as long as 18. Either way, it is a relatively short period of time when compared to a lifetime. You are making a major contribution in this generation and the generations to come. There is no need to prove your worth by running out and getting a job. True, there are aspects of being at home that are the pits, but that is also true in a career.

Pearl S. Buck writes beautifully while she affirms your place in society:

> Do I, who am a professional writer, believe that homemaking is the most important work in the world for a woman? Yes I do, and not only for others but for myself. As a writer, I know that it is essential for a woman to be a homemaker, and this is true whatever else she is.

> Woman, the housewife and homemaker creates more than she knows. While she sweeps and cleans and makes beds, while she cooks and washes and puts away, she is creating human beings. She is shaping dispositions and building character and making harmony . . .

> Seldom indeed do men and women rise

above the atmosphere of their childhood homes. They become rich and powerful, they may build houses very different from the one they first knew, but they carry within themselves the atmosphere of that first home . . . "[1]

One would not know that children are highly valued given the way many adults talk today. It is common to hear that they tie us down rather than to hear them called blessings, even if exhausting blessings!

But the question you need to examine, if indeed you are a homemaker, is *why* are you a homemaker? Is it because you have chosen to be? Is it because you feel it is expected of you? Is it because you are afraid and feel it is your only option?

If you are honest enough to admit fear, perhaps you need to use this stage in your life not only to be a homemaker but also as a time to gain new skills and further your education. If you feel you're too old, how old will you be in 10 years or so if you don't do it now?

Unfortunately, husbands die or leave and children grow up. Perhaps you would rather not face reality but that doesn't change the truth. In the Western world it is important for a woman to feel that if worse came to worse, she could care for herself and her family. Even though Jesus Christ settled the question of our value on Calvary, it is virtually impossible for a woman in our society to feel competent if she believes she has no skill by which she could earn a living.

Perhaps the basic issue is faith. Are you willing to affirm the promise that "you can do all things through Christ who strengthens you?" (see Phil. 4:13). Does that promise cover practical areas such as going back to school or trying a new interest?

Whatever you choose, be it homemaking, a career or both, never forget that you are in full-time Christian service. Perhaps you have chosen a career. Why did you make that choice? I sincerely hope you aren't searching for the happiness ever after fantasy. Perhaps your marriage is less than what you expected and so you are pursuing yet another fantasy. Please examine your heart and be sure you are not choosing a career to run away from home.

One of my favorite cartoons pictures a mother furiously paging through the want ads. Everything around her is in shambles and three children are hanging from the chandelier. Her husband's only question is, "Are you sure you want a career?" We've all had days like that, haven't we?

Perhaps you are working part-time to supplement the family income or full-time either by choice or because you are a single parent. Do you feel your career is helping to develop some of your God-given talents? If it is, what talents and gifts are being developed? There can be tremendous satisfaction in a career apart from the financial reward.

If your present career does not develop your gifts and talents, you may need to search for one that will. Perhaps your search will involve further education. Education is not likely to be viewed as an irritation if it is a means to the end of developing and using your gifts.

By this time you have a fairly comprehensive idea of your abilities, gifts, life-style and opportunities. What are you going to do with your lists?

2. Stimulate Your Dreams

A definition I particularly like for dreaming is "creative imagining." In the last few minutes you have focused on the raw material of you. Let's now focus on the person you would like to become. Terry Hershey refers to dreams as "mental images of who we can be as God's children. They allow us to see what God desires to do in and through us. They can be pictures of what God wants to make of us."[2]

What are your hopes for the future? Define them. Have you wanted to go back to school but just not had the courage? What about the dream of going into business for yourself? Have you wanted to learn a new language or perhaps increase your everyday vocabulary? What about those gorgeous goals you've been thinking about for such a long time? Where would you like to go? Dream a lot and get in touch with some of your fantasies. What do you want to do to further the kingdom of God on this planet?

I am not suggesting we all follow Pinocchio's lead and run off to pleasure island. Rather, I want you to get in touch with some of your unmet needs. Perhaps you feel that as a woman you are obligated to deny or repress those needs. Nothing could be further from the truth.

It seems most of us are constantly giving to others without examining some of our own needs. It is both necessary and possible to develop a plan to meet some of your needs without sacrificing the needs of others.

Pause and list some of your personal needs. While you're doing this may I share some of mine? I find a deep need for private, meditative time each day to worship my Lord. I need supportive, positive, intimate adult friends. I need to keep growing and learning. I have a very strong need for organization in my life and I find it necessary to take time away from my responsibilities for recreation. These are just a few of my needs, ones that I believe you can relate to.

Up to this time you have been letting your imagination run away with you. You have been brainstorming. The next step is to take this mass of information about who you are and begin to organize it. What is important to you must become clear in your imagination before it will take place in your life.

3. Start Prioritizing

What are the top three priorities that govern your life? List them below.

Priority 1:

Priority 2:

Priority 3:

Now that you have listed your priorities, go back and check last week's calendar. Did your activities fall under priority one, two or three? What happened?

If you're like I am, you will discover that unless you consistently check up on yourself, your week will consist of many good but rather unimportant activities if judged against your priority system.

Why don't you chart out an imaginary week, making sure that all entries fall under one of your three priorities. Would your life-style be slightly different than it is now?

If you live life without priorities you will find yourself a victim of everyone else's priorities. Is that what you wish?

Let me stress, once again, that we are God's representatives on planet Earth. We have been designed and appointed to live to the glory and praise of God. None of us want to simply fill up empty space with lots of good but misdirected activities. This automatically happens, I'm afraid, if we don't prioritize. Whatever we choose for our priorities eventually sets the framework for what we will become.

Does it seem overwhelming to start? Often it does, but if you dare to begin, you're miles ahead of many. "And who knows but that you have come to royal position for such a time as this?" (Esther 4:14, *NIV*).

4. Set Goals

My faith in Jesus Christ is central. All else flows from this—including my goals. The woman who sets low goals or no goals will achieve little or nothing. She will live on the isle that Denis Waitley refers to in this poem.

> There is an island fantasy
> A 'someday I'll' we'll never see
> When recession stops, inflation ceases
> Our mortgage is paid, our pay increases
> That someday I'll be where problems end
> Where every piece of mail is from a friend
> Where the children are sweet and
> already grown
> Where all the other nations can go it alone
> Where we all retire at forty-one
> Playing backgammon in the island sun
> Most unhappy people look to tomorrow
> To erase this day's heartache and sorrow
> They put happiness on 'lay away'
> And struggle through a blue today
> But happiness cannot be sought
> it can't be earned, it can't be bought
> Life's most important revelation
> is that the journey is more
> Than the destination.[3]

We need to establish goals, not excuses. Our life-style will be a matter of choice not chance. Let's live according to our priorities because Christ has declared us adequate and empowered us to touch our worlds meaningfully in His name. We do not set priorities and then goals because we are trying to prove our adequacy. The cross established that once and for all.

New Beginnings

First, write down three goals under each of your priorities, rating the goals according to their priority in your life. As you do this remember that your goals need to be realistic, attainable, time related and measurable. Perhaps one of your priorities is to deepen your relationship with the Lord. One of your goals could then be to set aside 30 minutes each day of the week, beginning today. Or perhaps one of your priorities is to keep growing. An attainable, measurable goal for you might be to read one book, every two weeks, for the next three months.

As you form some goals I suggest very strongly that you face your fears. What terrifies you the most? Is it returning to school? If it is, make a goal that confronts that fear. Register for one course in your area of interest at the closest college. Robert L. Stevenson encouraged us to fight our greatest fears or perish. Why not? I started to do this a few years ago and I have found it a liberating aspect to my life and my goal setting. The other day I heard a woman refer to herself as the original "chicken of the sea." If you qualify under that classification, make it a goal to enroll for the next swimming session at your local Y.W.C.A.! Remember, "God hath not given us the spirit of fear; but of power, and of love, and of a sound mind" (2 Tim. 1:7, *KJV*).

May I also suggest that you make it one of your goals to build up someone else's self-esteem. Perhaps your husband or your children need to confront an area of fear in their lives and overcome it. Is there something you can do

The Wheel of Choice

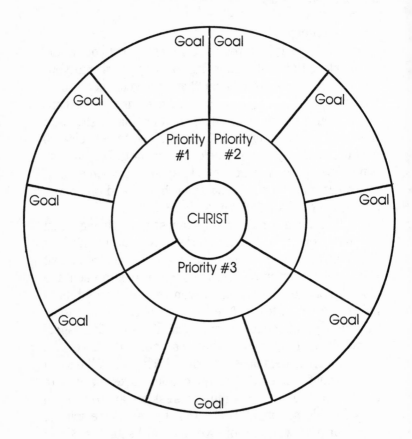

"A wise [woman] thinks ahead . . . it is pleasant to see plans develop" (Prov. 13, 19, *TLB*).

to facilitate their growth? Is there a phone call of affirmation you could make as part of your daily or weekly lifestyle? How is your letter writing coming?

Do you remember how you responded to the question I posed in chapter seven? What don't you like about yourself that you could change? Perhaps one of your responses can be listed under your goals.

Steps to Make My Goal a Reality

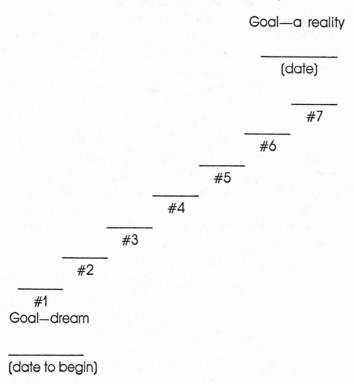

Goal—a reality

_____
(date)

_____
#7

_____
#6

_____
#5

_____
#4

_____
#3

_____
#2

_____
#1
Goal—dream

_____
(date to begin)

Second, choose the priority and goal of greatest importance to you.

Third, list some of the results from accomplishing this goal in your life.

Fourth, list some roadblocks you may encounter on the way to making this a reality in your life. Remember not to wait until all the solutions are obvious because you won't be walking by faith or even have the need to get started.

Fifth, develop a daily and weekly plan so your goal will become a realistic part of your life-style. Be certain you have broken your goal down into small enough steps so it is attainable. Now record your plan.

Happiness is a by-product of being committed to and involved in something you consider worthwhile. Until we acknowledge some of our own dreams and needs, without sacrificing the needs of those dear to us, we will never fully understand personal fulfillment, which is so essential to a healthy self-esteem.

Once your goal has been established, give it all you've got! Your goal is time-dated but if you don't achieve it within the time frame you originally established, revise your schedule rather than giving up your dream. Most people fail to meet their goals because they never set them in the first place.

Don't worry about your other priorities and goals, just work on the one of primary importance to you. When it becomes a reality in your life-style for at least a month, go back and choose another goal you would like to see come to life.

5. Speak Your Goals

Whether you are a homemaker, a career woman or both, home is in many ways the place you will succeed or fail. Home is a place to relax, but not to the extent that all organization goes out the window. Why don't you run your home as if you were self-employed, as if it were a small business?

If you have a full-time career I suggest that you arrange for some help, be it your family members or outside, to run your home efficiently. You are not a superwoman. You certainly don't want to fall into the habit pattern of working 24 hours a day, seven days a week. What jobs can you farm out?

If you are at home with young children, organization can be an immense help. Often your days are full of necessary but mundane chores. Your job description grows to fill the time you have available. Let's not be a victim of our homes. Let's choose to organize.

Over the years I have gained some valuable hints on home organization. I share eight with you here:

a. Make a list of those mundane chores that must be done daily. Divide them up between morning and evening chores. Do some yourself but don't forget to enlist your family's help.

b. Schedule routine weekly, monthly and quarterly activities. For example:

> weekly—grocery shopping, write letters to family
> monthly—vacuum under the furniture
> quarterly—wash windows, shampoo carpets

Put these on your calendar now. Perhaps Friday is the day you vacuum, Thursday the day you shop, Monday and Wednesday the day for laundry. Seasons of your life will vary, of course, so make up a schedule to fit your current life-style.

c. As I mentioned previously, I find it helpful to plan my week's activities all at one time. It is also the time to review my goals and see how I am progressing.

d. Plan your menus all at once. Only shop once a week if at all possible.

e. Have a master plan for your day. If you are a morning person, get up a little earlier to do some of your chores. If you are an owl, do them in the evening before you go to bed.

List the things you have to do and prioritize them. Ask yourself why you feel it is necessary to wash the dishes more than once a day, for example. Check up on your superwoman complex.

Make certain at least one activity you consider fulfilling is on that list. Do the most difficult or tedious activities when you are freshest. Don't use your best hour of the day to read the newspaper or sort through your mail.

f. Pray about interruptions at the beginning of your day so you are confident God has allowed them when they do come.

g. If you normally vacuum on Friday and for various reasons cannot get to it this week, don't add it to Saturday's schedule unless you're unable to ignore it one more day. Wait a week and complete the task the following Friday. Do you know how many years it has taken me to do that? I was the original Mrs. Clean but I used my chores as an excuse for the lack of time I spent on relationships. Please don't fall into that trap. You truly end up a *house*-wife, married to your house.

h. Schedule daily time for personal hygiene. If you are a full-time homemaker it is just as important to you as it is to the career woman to feel you look sharp. Daily exercise can certainly improve your perspective. You will look and feel more beautiful and alive.

7. Stick to It

A primary reason we are tempted to give up is other people. There is a small but significant number of people on this planet whose major goal in life is to encourage others to quit. But we don't have to listen, do we?

Beethoven rewrote his opera Fidelio four times, overcoming terrible failures and poor audience response. Each time he rewrote the opera it improved, until it finally became a masterpiece. Paul Erlich's cure for syphilis is coined 606: the magic bullet, because it was preceded by 605 failures.

There is a story Chuck Swindoll likes to tell about a couple of men who were working alongside the inventor, Thomas Edison. Weary to the point of exhaustion, one man sighed, "What a waste! We have tried no less than 700 experiments and nothing has worked. We are not a bit better off than when we started." With an optimistic twinkle in his eye, Edison quipped, "Oh yes, we are! We now know 700 things that won't work. We're closer than we've ever been before."

Is our Lord persistent? You know it! Does He ever stop loving? Does He ever stop forgiving? Does He ever remove hope from us? Never! If Christ is our Saviour we are promised that "He Who began a good work in you will continue until the day of Jesus Christ—right up to the time of His return—developing [that good work] and perfecting and bringing it to full completion in you" (Phil. 1:6, *AMP*). Since we are called to be "imitators of God" (Eph. 5:1) let's exercise our wills. Let's call on our self-discipline and stick with it.

8. Shun Comparisons

The problem with comparison is this: we always compare our worst with the other person's best. And more often than not their best is nothing more than our fantasy.

The first question I am usually asked when requested to do a seminar is, "Do you also sing?" I'll have you know that most of you wonderfully talented women who do both have ruined it for the rest of us!

Jesus calls us to cooperate with one another, not to

compare ourselves to one another. Some of us have been given one talent, some five and some 10. The number isn't the important issue. The questions to ask yourself are, *Am I shooting for the stars? Am I pursuing excellence with what God has given me?*

Jealousy is often a sign we have unmet personal needs. Instead of giving in to those negative emotions, why not reexamine the reasons for feeling the way we do. Instead of envying the trim figure on the girl next door, why don't you enroll in a personal exercise program?

9. Squelch Perfectionism

When perfectionism raises its ugly head in my life, it is a sign that, once again, I'm trying to earn God's favor. I need to remind myself that my adequacy has been declared. I have nothing to prove. May I shoot for the stars out of this sense of adequacy.

10. Shed Negativity

A woman once commented after one of my seminars that damage had resulted from the positive thinking movement. As true as this may be, what is our alternative? Does negativity and a critical spirit honor God? No way!

Your attitude toward life, your family and your job is vitally important because it will affect the atmosphere around you. A positive attitude is conducive to growth, will affect your health, has a predictive power and certainly is contagious. We are called to be facilitators of others' potential, to call forth the ability of others. Paul's goal was to present people to God. Can we do less? This is certainly impossible to accomplish with a negative spirit.

So, you haven't achieved your goal. You had the courage to try, didn't you? Often our biggest enemy is our own inertia. The question is not how you are going to finish but how you are running the race. Because we are human and not divine, we will face failure. A major step in our personal growth happens when we no longer defend our failures but ask the Lord to teach us what He has for us in the face of failure.

So you face a hurt. Why don't you turn it into a hurdle? Are you facing a crisis? Why don't you make it an opportunity? You failed yesterday? Why don't you turn your failure into a commitment to faithfulness? If you're disappointed, why don't you use your disappointment as an opportunity to exercise your self-discipline? Life is the ultimate do-it-to-yourself project in many ways.

If you pursue excellence by taking these 10 steps, a sense of personal satisfaction will result. Surround your priorities and goals with prayer and praise. With the psalmist, David, let's affirm Psalm 71:5-6,8 (*NIV*):

> For you have been my hope, O Sovereign Lord,
> my confidence since my youth.
> From birth I have relied on you;
> you brought me forth from my mother's womb
> I will ever praise you.
> My mouth is filled with your praise,
> Declaring your splendor all day long.

Moving Out

He was born and raised in poverty. He lived on what we would call the wrong side of the tracks. He had neither a wardrobe or a residence to which He could point with pride. He never became the confidant of the big shots of His day. He was the classic example of the common man. He belonged to an oppressed minority group—the Jews. Yet He never returned taunts with belligerency. He knew that insults and injustice could either turn Him into a better person—or a worse person. It all depended on Him. Using a positive attitude, He made negative social situations a way to turn Himself into a more sensitive, understanding, compassionate human being.

His family connection was simple and unpretentious. His father was a carpenter. The family lived in the poorest section of the poorly considered village of Nazareth. Yet He was proud of His family for they were good people.

He held no academic degrees, never travelled more than seventy-five miles from home, published no books, built no marble columned buildings. His only achievement was the building of a personal character and reputation that would be an inspiration to millions yet unborn. How did He become this kind of person? By specializing in the building of self-worth in persons that appeared worthless.

How did He build love in self-condemning people? He never called them sinners. Instead He gave them a new self-image, with words such as "You are the light of the world"—"You are the salt of the earth"—"Follow me and I will

make you fishers of men"—"Your sins are forgiven"—"If you have faith as a grain of mustard
seed, you can say to your mountain move—and
nothing will be impossible to you."

Even His shameful death failed to destroy His
strong self-assurance. To be crucified was to
die the most ignominious death possible—
naked, undraped, exposed in daylight to the
stares of men, women and children. To add further insult and indignity, He was hanged in the
company of two common thieves. Still He died,
as He lived, in dignity. How? By remembering
those around Him had problems. He was first of
all concerned about the executioners: how they
would hate themselves after the bloody deed
was all over. "Father, forgive them, for they
know not what they do," He prayed.

His spirit lives on today. He lives to tell you that
you too are a wonderful person when you allow
yourself to be used by God to save people from
self-degradation and to help raise them to
human dignity.[4]

Have you ever noticed that your own needs and problems seem less threatening when you are busy helping
someone else handle theirs? Have you noticed there is
less time to be critical of others when you are being honest
about yourself and those areas where you need to grow?
No longer is there a need in your life to take others apart
in order to justify your own need for improvement.
Because you are looking for and affirming the good in
yourself, your mission becomes one of building self-worth
in others.

You can now look for the good in others and tell them about it. This neither threatens you nor is used to manipulate them because you can now see the good in yourself, too. Your affirmations will not be focused just on what others do but also on who they are. They are significant and of great value in God's eyes and therefore they are significant in your eyes, too, apart from what they do. It is always possible you may be the closest thing to Jesus any of the people around you will ever see.

There is always something only you can do. If you are married your husband only has one wife—you. You have your neighbors, your children, your business acquaintances or your relatives. If you are single, you have a circle of friends unique to you. What one thing can you do in each of these people's lives to raise their self-dignity?

That's your assignment for the rest of your life. You will discover that loving the Father is done by loving those dear people in your life. You will discover what it means to be a woman, an interdependent woman, whose self-esteem comes as a result of being loved by God and whose self-concept is enhanced after loving and building self-esteem into the precious ones God has given you.

For the first time in many of your lives you will understand what it means to be free as a woman. You are:

Free to affirm your value but not free to base your value on your performance;

Free to develop your gifts but not to neglect their use in bettering your world;

Free to pursue excellence but not to prove your worth;

Free to soar like an eagle but not free to be puffed up with ego;

Free to define who you are but not to define
who I am;

Free to reach out to others but not to make
yourself responsible for their choices;

Free to love but not to lean;

Free to wear labels but not be defined by those
labels;

Free to be single but not free to be an island;

Free to be married but never to forget you are a
person;

Free to be a homemaker but not because there
are no other options;

Free to establish a career but not to escape to
utopia;

Free to lead but not free to lord it over others;

Free to affirm but not to manipulate, pretend or
blame;

Free to hold a child's hand but not to imprison
his spirit;

Free to submit but not to be a doormat;
Free to define your own needs and dreams and
see them become reality but not at the expense
of those you care for;

Free to accept your femininity but not free to deny, degrade or imitate someone's masculinity;

Free to realize your equality but not to use it as an excuse for refusing to serve;

Free to talk but not at the expense of listening;

Free to believe but not without asking questions;

Free to ask questions but not free to expect all the answers;

Free to be positive but not free to be a pollyanna;

Free to laugh but never at the expense of another;

Free to be vulnerable but not free to force me to be;

Free to be creative but not to the exclusion of relationships;

Free to be hospitable but not for the purpose of showing off;

Free to pray but not free to procrastinate;

Free to be involved but not free to be consumed by business;

Free to face issues but not to lose sight of priorities;

Free to state your beliefs but not free to harbor anger and bitterness when others' beliefs are different from yours;

Free to face intimidation but not free to be intimidated;

Free to dream but not to forget that the dreams come from God;

Free to fail but not to abandon your dreams because you failed;

Free to be interdependent but not without first examining and rejecting the options of dependence and independence;

Free to see living as a privilege, not as a problem.

For the first time in many of your lives you are free to be yourself. You are free as an interdependent woman. Let's never choose self-imposed bondage again.

Remember always that *You* are God's way of being creative!

To God be the glory!

Notes

Chapter 1

1. From *A Woman's Worth* by Elaine Stedman, copyright © 1976; used by permission of Word Books, Publisher, Waco, Texas 76796.
2. From *There's a Lot More to Health Than Not Being Sick* by Bruce Larson, copyright © 1981; used by permission of Word Books, Publisher, Waco, Texas 76796.

Chapter 2

1. From *Why Am I Afraid to Tell You Who I Am?* by John Powell, S.J. © 1969 Argus Communications, a division of DLM, Inc., Allen, Texas 75002. Used by permission.
2. © Real People Press 1969. All rights reserved. Used by permission.

Chapter 3

1. Jim and Sally Conway, *Women in Mid-Life Crisis,* Copyright © 1983 by Jim and Sally Conway, Tyndale House Publishers, Inc. Used by permission.

2. Judy Haralson, "Freedom," *Faith at Work Magazine* (September, 1975). Used by permission.

3. From *There's a Lot More to Health Than Not Being Sick* by Bruce Larson, copyright © 1981; used by permission of Word Books, Publisher, Waco, Texas 76796.

4. Ibid.

5. Ibid.

6. William M. Kinnaird, *Joy Comes with the Morning,* Word Books, Waco, Texas 1979. Used by permission.

Chapter 4

1. Excerpt from START LOVING: THE MIRACLE OF FORGIVING by Colleen Townsend Evans. Copyright © 1976 by Colleen Townsend Evans and Laura Hobe. Reprinted by permission of Doubleday and Company, Inc.

2. *431 Quotes* by Henrietta C. Mears. © Copyright 1970, Regal Books, Ventura, California 93006. Used by permission.

3. From *There's a Lot More to Health Than Not Being Sick* by Bruce Larson, copyright © 1981; used by permission of Word Books, Publisher, Waco, Texas 76796.

4. Author unknown.

Chapter 5

1. "Because God Loves Me" by Dick Dickenson. Taken from *Improving Your Self Image* © 1983 Harvest House Publishers, Eugene, Oregon 97402. Used by permission.

2. If you'd like to learn more about this remarkable young lady and her great big God, I suggest *Michelle* by Carolyn E. Phillips, published by Regal Books, a Division of GL Publications, Ventura, California 93006.

Chapter 6

1. Walter Tubbs, "Beyond Perls." Journal of Humanistic Psychology, 12 (Fall 1972), p. 5.

Chapter 7

1. From SEEDS OF GREATNESS by Denis Waitley copyright © 1983 by Denis Waitley, Inc. Published by Fleming H. Revell Company. Used by permission.

Chapter 8

1. From the book, GET THE BEST FROM YOURSELF by Nido R. Qubein © 1983 by Nido R. Qubein. Published by Prentice-Hall, Inc., Englewood Cliffs, NJ 07632. Used by permission.

Chapter 9

1. From SEEDS OF GREATNESS by Denis Waitley copyright © 1983 by Denis Waitley, Inc. Published by Fleming H. Revell Company. Used by permission.
2. Anonymous
3. Leo Buscaglia, *Living, Loving and Learning* (NY: Fawcett, 1983), pp. 263-264. Used by permission.
4. Terry Hershey, *Beginning Again: Life After the Relationship Ends* (Laguna Hills, CA: Merit Books, 1984), p. 116.
5. From SEEDS OF GREATNESS by Denis Waitley copyright © 1983 by Denis Waitley, Inc. Published by Fleming H. Revell Company. Used by permission.
6. William M. Kinnaird, *Joy Comes with the Morning,* Word Books, Waco, Texas 1979. Used by permission.

Chapter 10

1. From *Improving Your Serve* by Charles R. Swindoll, copyright © 1982, used by permission of Word Books, Publisher, Waco, Texas 76796.
2. Reprinted from *To God with Love* by Dottie Versteeg. Copyright © 1980 Review and Herald Publishing Association. Used by permission.

Chapter 11

1. Taken from HEIRS TOGETHER, by Patricia Gundry. Copyright © 1980 by The Zondervan Corporation. Used by permission.
2. From *A Woman's Worth* by Elaine Stedman, copyright © 1976; used by permission of Word Books, Publisher, Waco, Texas 76796.
3. John Sterner, *How to Become Super-Spiritual or Kill Yourself Trying* (Nashville: Abingdon, 1982), p. 44. Used by permission.
4. Diagram reprinted by permission from the book, *When You Don't Agree* by James G. T. Fairfield, copyright by Herald Press, Scottdale, Pa. 15683.
5. Taken from HEIRS TOGETHER, by Patricia Gundry. Copyright © 1980 by The Zondervan Corporation. Used by permission.
6. From *Beyond Assertiveness* by John Paul and David Augsburger, copyright © 1980; used by permission of Word Books, Publisher, Waco, Texas 76796.
7. Reprinted by permission from HOW AM I SUPPOSED TO LOVE MYSELF? by Phoebe Cranor, published and copyright 1979, Bethany House Publishers, Minneapolis, MN 55438.
8. The world "liberation" refers to our freedom in Jesus Christ. We find true freedom only when bound to our Saviour and we *need* to be liberated into the awareness of what our freedom in Him means. I do not

agree with society's definition of liberation. Women who do agree with this definition are bound in hostility, bitterness and estranged relationships because they are reacting against dependency.

9. From IMAGES: WOMEN IN TRANSITION, compiled by Janice Grana, copyright © 1976 by The Upper Room. Used by permission of the publisher.

10. Mary Carolyn Davies, (public domain).

Chapter 12

1. Pearl S. Buck, *To My Daughters, with Love* (NY: John Day Company, 1967), pp. 184-186.

2. Terry Hershey, *Beginning Again: Life After the Relationship Ends* (Laguna Hills, CA: Merit Books, 1984), pp. 25-26.

3. From SEEDS OF GREATNESS by Denis Waitley copyright © 1983 by Denis Waitley, Inc. Published by Fleming H. Revell Company. Used by permission.

4. From *Self-Esteem: The New Reformation* by Robert H. Schuller, copyright © 1982; used by permission of Word Books, Publisher, Waco, Texas 76796.